access to history

Crisis in the Middle East: Israel and the Arab States 1945–2007

Michael Scott-Baumann

HODDER
EDUCATION

AN HACHETTE UK COMPANY

The publishers would like to thank the following individuals, institutions and companies for permission to reproduce copyright illustrations in this book: © Jon Arnold/JAI/Corbis, page 12; © Bettmann/Corbis, pages 62, 78; Peter Brookes, *The Times*, 28 March 2004, British Cartoon Archive, University of Kent © NI Syndication, page 105; Sahm Doherty/Time Life Pictures/Getty Images, page 54; © Express Newspapers, page 19; Fox Photos/Getty Images, page 43; © Illingworth, *Daily Mail*, 22 September 1947, Llyfrgell Genedlaethol Cymru/National Library of Wales (NLW: Illingworth collection, ILW01311), Associated Newspapers/Solo Syndication, page 31; © INA/epa/Corbis, page 115; Keystone/Getty Images, page 69; Bashar Nazal/AFP/Getty Images, page 103; © Alain Nogues/CORBIS SYGMA, pages 80, 135; © Reuters/CORBIS, pages 94, 147; © Michel Setboun/Corbis, page 119; Sipa Press/Rex Features, page 84; STF/AFP/Getty Images, pages 39, 73; © Peter Turnley/CORBIS, page 106; © David H. Wells/CORBIS, page 88; Khalid Zighari/AP/PA Photos, pages 99, 100.

The publishers would like to acknowledge use of the following extracts: Cambridge University Press for an extract from *A History of Modern Palestine* by Ilan Pappe, 2004; Interlink Publishing Group for an extract from *The Palestinians* by Jonathan Dimbleby, 1979; I.B. Tauris for an extract from *A Modern History of the Kurds* by D. McDowall, 2004; Vintage Books for an extract from *The Arab-Israeli Wars: War and Peace in the Middle East* by C. Herzog, 1982.

The publishers would also like to thank the following for permission to reproduce material in this book: 'Horror in the Market Place', by Julian Borger, *The Guardian*, 31 July 1997, Copyright Guardian News & Media Ltd 1997, page 98.

Every effort has been made to trace all copyright holders, but if any have been inadvertently overlooked the Publishers will be pleased to make the necessary arrangements at the first opportunity.

Hachette UK's policy is to use papers that are natural, renewable and recyclable products and made from wood grown in sustainable forests. The logging and manufacturing processes are expected to conform to the environmental regulations of the country of origin.

Orders: please contact Bookpoint Ltd, 130 Milton Park, Abingdon, Oxon OX14 4SB. Telephone: (44) 01235 827720. Fax: (44) 01235 400454. Lines are open 9.00–5.00, Monday to Saturday, with a 24-hour message answering service. Visit our website at www.hoddereducation.co.uk

© Michael Scott-Baumann 2009
First published in 2009 by
Hodder Education,
An Hachette UK Company
338 Euston Road
London NW1 3BH

Impression number   7
Year   2013 2012

Cover photo shows Arab Americans marching against Israel's bombing of Lebanon, Jim West/Alamy
Typeset in 10/12pt Baskerville and produced by Gray Publishing, Tunbridge Wells
Printed and bound by CPI Group (UK) Ltd, Croydon, CR0 4YY

A catalogue record for this title is available from the British Library.

ISBN: 978 0340 966 587

Contents

Dedication

Keith Randell (1943–2002)

The *Access to History* series was conceived and developed by Keith, who created a series to 'cater for students as they are, not as we might wish them to be'. He leaves a living legacy of a series that for over 20 years has provided a trusted, stimulating and well-loved accompaniment to post-16 study. Our aim with these new editions is to continue to offer students the best possible support for their studies.

Introduction: The Scope of the Book

The term 'Middle East' is commonly used to refer to the area incorporating Israel and surrounding Arab states. It includes the countries that share borders with Israel – Egypt, Jordan, Syria and Lebanon – and countries such as Iraq and Saudi Arabia. Iran is not usually included because it is further east and because it is not Arab or Arabic speaking. However, it is included in Chapter 7 of this book because, in the past 30 years, it has had a big impact on the politics of the region.

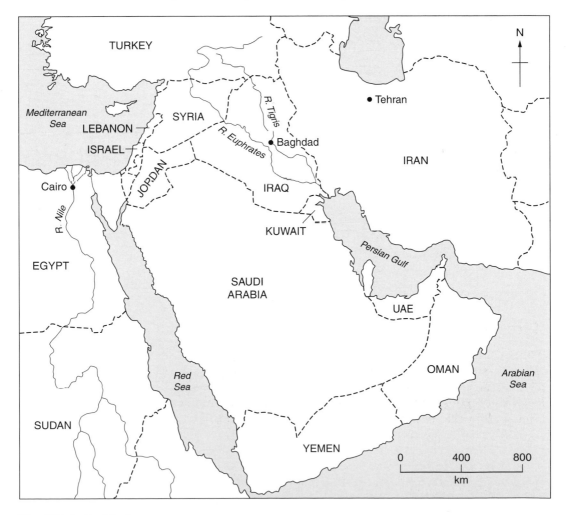

The Middle East today.

The Middle East has been of huge importance in human history. It includes the two areas of oldest human civilisation: that along the Nile in Egypt and the area between the two rivers, the Tigris and the Euphrates, in today's Iraq. It is also the birthplace of three major world religions: Judaism, Christianity and Islam. The area at the centre of the Middle East (Israel/Palestine) is often referred to as the 'Holy Land'.

In the past hundred years, the Middle East has most commonly been associated with conflict, often over land or oil, and who controls it. Much of this strife has arisen over the creation of the Jewish state of Israel out of the land of Palestine in 1948. Since then there have been several wars between Israel and its Arab neighbours. Today, the conflict between Israel and the Palestinian Arabs remains at the core of so many crises in the Middle East.

The Arab–Israeli conflict is the main focus of this book but it also examines:

- Arab nationalism, especially in Egypt and Syria
- the Islamic revolution in Iran in 1979
- the causes and consequences of three wars involving Iraq
- the growth of political Islam and Islamic fundamentalism.

1 Jews, Arabs and the British 1900–39

1 | The Jewish Claim to Palestine

The expulsion of the Jews from Palestine

Key question
What was the Jewish claim to Palestine?

The Jewish people lived in the land of Palestine (see map on page 9) from about 1500 BC. In the time of Jesus – first century AD – Palestine was ruled by the Romans. In AD 70 and again in AD 135 the Jews rebelled against their Roman rulers. Roman soldiers crushed both revolts, destroyed the Jewish temple, the city of Jerusalem and expelled most of the Jews. Many thousands fled to neighbouring countries and, over the next 200 years, they settled in almost every part of the Roman Empire, particularly in southern Europe. The Jews thus became a scattered people and only a few thousand remained in Palestine. Many of those who lived in the **diaspora** became merchants and farmers, bankers and craftsmen. Some became wealthy and even gained important positions in the governments of the new lands in which they

Key term
Diaspora
The dispersal of Jews in many different parts of the world.

lived. Nevertheless, Jewish people kept alive their religious traditions, building **synagogues** for worship and celebrating Jewish festivals and holy days.

Anti-Semitism in Europe

The Jews were often persecuted. Almost all Europeans were Christians and they often forced the Jews to live in separate areas. The Jews were not allowed to vote or even to buy their own land. Then, when **persecution** increased in the Middle Ages, the Jews were expelled from much of western Europe and many settled in Russia and Poland.

In the nineteenth century, the country with the largest Jewish population was Russia. When the Tsar (emperor) was assassinated in 1881, there were a lot of anti-Jewish riots. Many people in the government blamed the Jews for the assassination and the new Tsar's government encouraged the persecution of the Jews. Synagogues were burnt down, Jewish homes were attacked and thousands of Jews were killed. Many Russian Jews fled to western Europe and the USA. But, even there, Jews often found that they were not treated as equals and that they were sometimes suspected of being disloyal or untrustworthy. All these various forms of anti-Jewish behaviour are known as **anti-Semitism**.

In 1896, Theodor Herzl, an Austrian Jew living in Paris, published a book entitled *The Jewish State*. In it, he wrote:

> Are we to get out now, and where to? Or may we remain, and how long? Let us first settle the point of staying where we are now. Can we hope for better days? I say we cannot hope for change in the current feeling. Even if we were as near the hearts of princes as are their other subjects, they could not protect us. They would only feed popular hatred by showing us too much favour.

He said his plan was 'perfectly simple': the Jews were to be granted 'a portion of the globe large enough to satisfy the rightful requirements of a nation'.

> We must not imagine the departure of the Jews to be a sudden one. It will be gradual, continuous and will cover many decades. The poorest will go first to cultivate the soil.
> They will construct roads, bridges, railways and telegraph installations, regulate rivers and build their own dwellings; their labour will create trade, trade will create markets and markets will attract new settlers.

'Next year in Jerusalem'

For hundreds of years Jews dreamt and prayed that they would be able to celebrate 'Next Year in Jerusalem'. By the beginning of the twentieth century, an increasing number of Jews in Europe and the USA were, like Herzl, demanding a Jewish national home. By 1914, when the First World War broke out, these people were all agreed that this homeland would have to be in Palestine. This was the **'Promised Land'**, where the Jews (or **Israelites**) had

Key terms

Synagogue
A building where Jews worship.

Persecution
Punishment or cruel treatment, often because of ethnicity or religion.

Anti-Semitism
Feelings or actions showing prejudice or hatred towards the Jews.

'Promised Land'
The land of Palestine (which Jews believed God had promised to them).

Israelites
The name by which Jews were known in ancient times, hence the 'Land of Israel' was their Promised Land.

Key term

Zionists
Those who advocated the creation of a Jewish homeland and, later, an independent state, in Palestine.

Key question
What was the importance of the Balfour Declaration?

Key date

Balfour Declaration: 1917

lived some 2000 years before and where several thousands still remained.

Not all Jews wanted to return to the 'Land of Israel'. Most wanted to stay where they were: in France, Britain, Germany, Russia or wherever they were living, but a small number, especially from Russia, made their way to Palestine. They bought land there and started to farm and build homes. These people and all those who believed in a Jewish national homeland were called **Zionists** after Mount Zion, a mountain near Jerusalem. Between 1880 and 1914, 60,000 Zionists settled in Palestine.

The Balfour Declaration 1917

During the First World War, British Zionists, led by Chaim Weizmann, worked hard to win the support of the British government for a Jewish homeland. In 1917, they received a great boost. The British were bogged down in the fighting with Germany and they were very keen to bring the USA into the war. They believed that the Jews in America could influence their government's actions. This was one of the reasons why the British government declared its support for a Jewish homeland in Palestine. The declaration was made in the form of a letter to Lord Rothschild, a leading British Jew, in November 1917. It became known as the 'Balfour Declaration' because it was signed by the British Foreign Secretary, Lord Balfour. It stated:

> Foreign Office
> December 2nd, 1917
>
> Dear Lord Rothschild,
>
> I have much pleasure in expressing to you, on behalf of His Majesty's Government, the following declaration of sympathy with Jewish Zionist ambitions. This has been approved by the Cabinet.
> 'His Majesty's Government view with favour the establishment in Palestine of a national home for the Jewish people. The Government will make every effort to help bring this about. It is clearly understood that nothing shall be done which may harm the civil and religious rights of existing non-Jewish communities in Palestine, or the rights and political status enjoyed by Jews in any other country.'
> I should be grateful if you would bring this declaration to the knowledge of the Zionist Federation.
>
> [Signed by Lord Balfour]

The British were very careful with their wording of the declaration. They expressed their support for a Jewish homeland, not a state but, for the next 30 years, many Jews regarded the declaration as a promise from the British government to help set up a Jewish state.

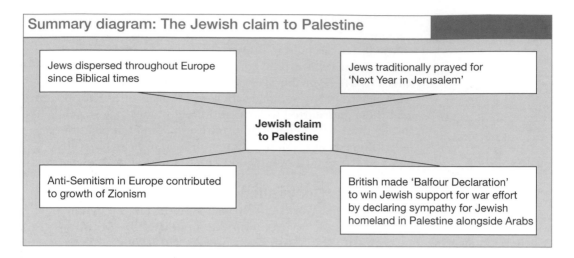

Summary diagram: The Jewish claim to Palestine

Jews dispersed throughout Europe since Biblical times

Jews traditionally prayed for 'Next Year in Jerusalem'

Jewish claim to Palestine

Anti-Semitism in Europe contributed to growth of Zionism

British made 'Balfour Declaration' to win Jewish support for war effort by declaring sympathy for Jewish homeland in Palestine alongside Arabs

2 | The Arab Claim to Palestine

Originally, the Arabs lived in the desert area which is today mostly Saudi Arabia (see map on page 9). They all spoke the same language, Arabic. In the seventh century AD, most of the Arabs were converted to the religion of Islam. They became followers of **Muhammad** and became known as Muslims. From their homeland in Arabia, they swept across the Middle East and north Africa in the seventh and eighth centuries, spreading their new religion and their language. Palestine was one of the countries they took over. Today, the Arabs form the majority of the population in the Middle East and all speak the same language, Arabic.

In the Middle Ages, the Muslim Arabs produced one of the world's richest and most powerful civilisations. They made important discoveries in mathematics and medicine while their mosques are still some of the most beautiful buildings in the world. Their merchants bought and sold goods in Europe, Africa and Asia, and their lands grew rich. Then, in the sixteenth century, the **Ottoman** Turks (who were also Muslims but not Arabs) conquered much of the Middle East. The Arabs were forced to pay taxes and provide soldiers for their Turkish masters. In the late nineteenth century the Arabs tried several times to remove their Turkish rulers. Their aim was to re-establish Arab rule in the Middle East, including Palestine. In 1913, the first Arab National Congress was held and, a year later, the Arab Nationalist Manifesto was published. This called for independence from Turkey and unity among the Arabs:

> Arise, O ye Arabs! Take out the sword from the scabbard. Do not let an oppressive tyrant [Turkey], who only despises you, remain in your country; cleanse your country from those who show their hatred to you, to your race and to your language.
>
> O ye Arabs! You all dwell in one land, you speak one language, so be also one nation and one land.
>
> Do not become divided amongst yourselves.

Key question
What was the Arab claim to Palestine?

Key terms

Muhammad
Born in the Arabian city of Mecca in AD 572. For Muslims, he is the messenger and prophet of God.

Ottoman
The name of the Turkish dynasty, named after its founder, Osman. In the sixteenth century, the Turkish empire conquered much of south-east Europe and the Middle East.

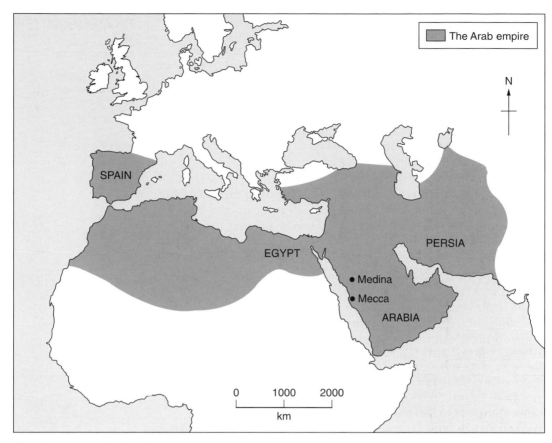

The Arab empire in the eighth century.

The Arabs and the First World War

Key question
To what extent was the First World War a turning point in the struggle for Arab independence?

The First World War was a turning point in the Arab struggle for independence as well as in the Jewish struggle for a homeland. Again it was the British who played a crucial role. Turkey fought on the German side against Britain and its allies. The British were afraid that their supplies of oil from Persia (or Iran as it is known today) might be cut off by the Turks. The British navy was beginning to make more use of oil, as opposed to coal, to fuel its ships at this time. So they decided to encourage the Arabs to rebel against their Turkish rulers and seek independence.

The British **High Commissioner** in Egypt, Sir Herbert McMahon, exchanged several letters with Hussein, the Sharif of Mecca, in 1915. Hussein was Guardian of Mecca and Medina, the two holy sites of Islam (in what is today Saudi Arabia). As such, he was the most important Arab Muslim leader. McMahon promised Hussein that if the Arabs fought against the Turks:

Key term

High Commissioner
The most senior diplomat, like an ambassador, representing the British government.

Key date

McMahon–Hussein letters: 1915

> Great Britain is prepared to recognise and support the independence of the Arabs. When the situation allows, Great Britain will assist the Arabs to establish what may appear to be the most suitable forms of government in those various territories.

In 1916 an Arab army was raised and led by Prince Faisal, the son of the Sharif of Mecca. The army blew up Turkish trains and disrupted the flow of military supplies to the Turkish soldiers. This became known as the Arab Revolt. The activities of this Arab army are well known because an English army intelligence officer, Major T.E. Lawrence, who became known in Britain as 'Lawrence of Arabia', fought with the Arabs. In 1918, Faisal and his Arab soldiers were allowed by the British to march in and take the city of Damascus, in Syria, from the Turks.

The Arab Revolt: 1916

Sykes–Picot Agreement: 1916

Britain granted mandate over Palestine: 1919

Key dates

The Sykes–Picot Agreement 1916

The Arabs felt that they had fought for their independence from the Turks and now deserved complete self-government. Arab leaders were therefore angered when they heard that Britain and France had secretly agreed, in 1916, to carve up Turkey's Arab lands after the war and share them out between themselves. This agreement is known as the Sykes–Picot Agreement after the British and French politicians who made it. Under the agreement, some Arab land would be directly ruled by Britain or France while the rest would be Arab states with either Britain or France having some indirect control over them.

Why did the British make this agreement?

- The war in Europe (against Germany) was not going well and it was vital for Britain to maintain a strong alliance with France, its main ally in the war.
- Both Britain and France had extensive trading links with the Middle East.
- Britain wanted to protect the Suez Canal, which was jointly owned and operated with the French. The Canal was the main route to Britain's empire in India and to the recently discovered oilfields in the Persian Gulf (see map on page 9). Britain already controlled Egypt and saw Palestine as an additional buffer zone to protect the Canal and the route to the east.

To sum up, Britain and France wished to maintain their power and influence in the Middle East and they saw the Sykes–Picot Agreement as an important step to achieving this.

Mandate
An order or command, in this case from the League of Nations, giving Britain and France control of Arab lands previously ruled by Turkey. Britain and France were to prepare the Arab lands for eventual self-government.

Key term

British and French mandates in the Middle East

Arab fears were confirmed in 1919. In the Treaty of Versailles, which followed the end of the First World War, Britain and France were given **mandates**, or orders, to govern certain countries in the Middle East until the Arab people were considered ready to govern themselves. Britain was given mandates over Palestine, Transjordan (later known as Jordan) and Iraq, and British troops and government officials took control of these lands. France was granted mandates over Syria and Lebanon and sent troops in to take control.

Key question
Why did Britain and France want mandates in the Middle East?

Lawrence ('Lawrence of Arabia') felt that Hussein, the Sharif of Mecca, had been humiliated by the Sykes–Picot Agreement and the subsequent mandates. Hussein was head of the Hashemite family who were descended from the Prophet Muhammad. At the end of the war, Lawrence had advised the British government to establish Hussein's son, Faisal, as King of Syria. However, Syria was a French mandate and the British, now the strongest power in the Middle East, seemed to attach more importance to their alliance with France than their promises to Hussein. In 1921, the British allowed French forces to invade Syria and expel Faisal from the throne he had held for two years.

Instead, the British made Faisal King of Iraq and recognised his older brother, Abdullah, as the ruler of Transjordan. (He became King in 1946.) The two Hashemite princes thus became rulers of the semi-independent Arab states of Iraq and Transjordan, both of which were British mandates. These countries became two of the main pillars of Britain's empire in the Middle East after the First World War.

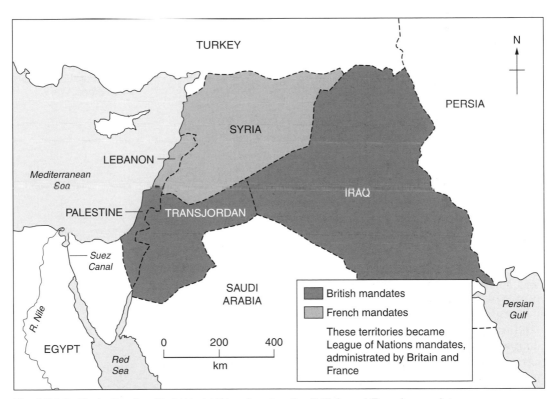

The Middle East after the First World War showing the British and French mandates.

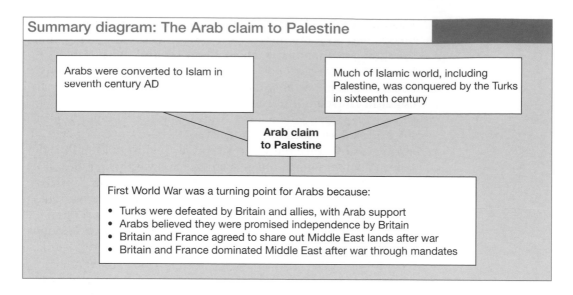

Summary diagram: The Arab claim to Palestine

Arabs were converted to Islam in seventh century AD

Much of Islamic world, including Palestine, was conquered by the Turks in sixteenth century

Arab claim to Palestine

First World War was a turning point for Arabs because:

- Turks were defeated by Britain and allies, with Arab support
- Arabs believed they were promised independence by Britain
- Britain and France agreed to share out Middle East lands after war
- Britain and France dominated Middle East after war through mandates

3 | British Rule in Palestine 1919–39

In 1917 British troops entered Jerusalem, the capital of Palestine, driving out the Turks. Two years later Britain was given a mandate to govern Palestine and, for the next 30 years, the British government was to rule the country. In 1922 the League of Nations confirmed that:

> Britain shall be responsible for placing the country under such political, administrative and economic conditions as will secure the establishment of the Jewish national home and the development of self-governing institutions, and also for safeguarding the civil and religious rights of all the inhabitants of Palestine no matter what their race or religion.

The Arabs of Palestine felt that they had simply exchanged Turkish rulers for British ones. Like the Arabs of Syria and Iraq, they were frustrated and disappointed that they had not been given their independence. They were even more angered by increasing Jewish immigration and the fact that Jews were buying land in 'their' country. Much of the land was bought from Arab landowners, many of whom were absentee landlords living in the cities. Furthermore, Arabs who had worked on the land, as tenants, were evicted because, very often, only Jews were employed to work on Jewish farms. The Jews only bought land in a few areas of Palestine but, in these areas, the Arabs claimed they were being driven out. They also accused the British of being pro-Zionist. The British High Commissioner in Palestine, Sir Herbert Samuel, was Jewish. To the Arabs, the British seemed to be favouring the Jews.

At the Paris peace conference, held at Versailles, in 1919, the British Zionist, Chaim Weizmann was asked what was meant by a Jewish national home. He replied: 'To make Palestine as Jewish as England is English'. But he did not speak openly of a Jewish

Key question
Why were Palestinian Arabs angry about Jews immigrating to Palestine after the First World War?

'state' so as not to be accused of trying to make the Jewish minority become the masters of the Arab majority. He knew there was a limit to how far he could push the British. As a leading British Zionist, he knew that if the Jewish national home was to survive it needed the continued support of the British rulers of Palestine.

Arab–Jewish riots

Ever since the first Jewish settlers had arrived in Palestine from Russia in 1882, there had been attacks on Jewish property and people. In 1921 violence on a massive scale erupted in the town of Jaffa (see the map below), a busy sea port. Jaffa was different from other Arab coastal towns because it was the main port of arrival for Jewish immigrants. Just to the north of the town was Tel Aviv, the largest Jewish settlement in Palestine. In 1921 riots erupted in Tel Aviv between rival Jewish groups. The fighting spread into Arab Jaffa and led to Arab attacks on Jews and their property. After two days of rioting, 200 Jews and 120 Arabs were dead or wounded.

The British authorities immediately stopped all Jewish immigration and the Palestinian Arabs were told that only a part of Palestine was to be made into a Jewish national home. Soon afterwards immigration began again but the British insisted it would be limited. The Arabs asked the British government to make Palestine independent as they hoped that the Arab majority

The main areas of Jewish settlement in Palestine in the 1920s.

would be able to dominate the Jewish minority. When Winston Churchill, a government minister, visited Palestine in 1921, a group of Arab leaders asked him to refute the Balfour Declaration and stop immigration. Churchill replied: 'You ask me to reject the Balfour Declaration and to stop immigration. This is not in my power and it is not my wish.'

The British government seemed unable to satisfy either Jews or Arabs in Palestine. The rate of immigration slowed down in the 1920s, and yet the Jewish population still doubled in the 10 years after the war. By 1929 there were a million Arabs and 160,000 Jews living in Palestine whereas, in 1919, there had only been 60,000 Jews (see the bar graph on page 13).

In 1929 violence erupted again. This time it started in the city of Jerusalem, which is a holy city for both Muslims and Jews. In the 1920s there was continuous tension in the city, particularly over who controlled the holy places (which you can see in the photograph). In August 1929, riots broke out and Arab crowds attacked Jews inside and outside the city. The attacks spread throughout Palestine and 133 Jews were killed over four days. One hundred and sixteen Arabs were also killed, mostly by the British police.

Two of the most holy places are shown in this photograph. The Mosque of the Dome of the Rock was built on the rock from which Muslims believe that Muhammad rose to heaven. Just below it, in the foreground, is the Western or 'Wailing' Wall, which Jews believe to be the last remaining part of the ancient Jewish Temple.

Key question
Why did British rule
lead to an Arab
rebellion in Palestine?

Key dates

Hitler came to power
in Germany: 1933

Arab Rebellion:
1936–9

Nazi anti-Semitism and Jewish immigration

Similar outbreaks of violence, although not so widespread,
continued in the early 1930s, especially after 1933. In that year
Adolf Hitler came to power in Germany and Nazi anti-Semitism
drove many Jews abroad. Thousands fled to Palestine and by
1939 there were nearly 450,000 Jews in the country. Tension
remained high and British government reports all came to the
same conclusion: the Arabs were afraid of losing their country as
more and more of them became 'landless and discontented'.

The British therefore planned to restrict immigration and land
sales. This caused uproar among the Jews in Europe and the USA
as well as in Palestine, so the plan was put aside. The British were
in an impossible position: if they allowed unrestricted
immigration, Arab fears and violence would increase. But if they
stopped or controlled immigration, the world would accuse them
of inhumanity, of not caring for the Jews who were being
persecuted by the Nazis.

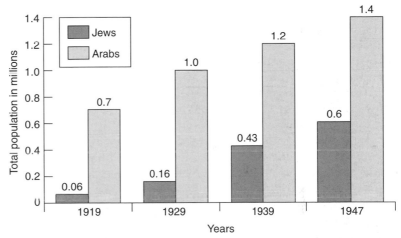

Jewish and Arab populations in Palestine, 1919–47.

The Arab Rebellion 1936–9

In April 1936 widespread fighting broke out as armed Arab bands
attacked Jewish settlements. Within a month, over 20 Jews had
been killed. By mid-summer, Palestine was caught up in a civil
war that was to last for three years and cost hundreds of lives. The
British responded harshly. They hanged several Arab leaders and
destroyed houses suspected of containing Arab terrorists or arms.
They also helped to train and organise the Jewish Defence Force,
the **Haganah**.

Orde Wingate was a British officer who trained Jewish squads
to attack Arab villages during the rebellion. He was an effective
military leader, but also a very cruel one.

Key term

Haganah
The Jewish Defence
Force, which was set
up in the 1920s and
was later to form
the basis of the
Israeli army.

> Wingate went up to the four Arab prisoners. He said in Arabic, 'You
> have arms in the village. Where have you hidden them?' The Arabs
> shook their heads. Wingate reached down and took sand from the

ground. He thrust it into the mouth of the first Arab and pushed it down until he puked. 'Now', he said, 'Where have you hidden the arms?' Still they shook their heads. Wingate turned to one of the Jews and, pointing to the coughing Arab, said, 'Shoot this man'. The Jew looked at him and hesitated. Wingate said in a tense voice, 'Did you hear? Shoot this man.' The Jew shot the Arab. The others stared in horror at the dead body. The Jewish boys looked in silence. 'Now speak,' said Wingate. They spoke.

The Peel Commission 1937

In 1937, the British government set up an inquiry, led by Lord Peel. In their report, the Peel Commission recommended the **partition** of Palestine into two separate states, one Jewish and the other Arab. The Arabs rejected the plan while the Jews wanted more land than they were allocated under it. The fighting continued and, eventually, with the help of more troops, better weapons and transport, the British forces were able to regain control of Palestine.

By 1939, when the rebellion ended, the British government had given up all further ideas of partition. War was approaching and Britain feared the growth of friendship between Arab leaders and Germany. Britain needed to keep the Arab countries on their side so that oil supplies from the Middle East would continue to reach Britain. The government issued a special report called a **White Paper**. This declared that Britain wanted an independent Palestine within 10 years. This would be neither a Jewish state nor an Arab one, but one in which Arabs and Jews shared responsibility for governing the country. Meanwhile, Britain would continue to rule Palestine. The White Paper also said that Britain would restrict Jewish immigration:

> For each of the next five years a limit of 10,000 Jewish immigrants will be allowed apart from a special quota in the near future of 25,000 refugees as a contribution to the solution of the Jewish refugee problem.
>
> After the period of five years no further Jewish immigration will be permitted unless the Arabs are prepared to agree to it.

Not surprisingly, the Jews were furious.

Key question
Why did the British decide on, and later reject, the partition of Palestine?

Partition
Division into two or more parts.

White Paper
A government document making recommendations for discussion.

Peel Commission recommended partition of Palestine: 1937

British government White Paper: 1939

Summary diagram: British rule in Palestine 1919–39

British rule imposed on Palestine after war

Jewish immigration in 1920s led to:
- Arabs losing land
- outbreaks of Arab–Jewish violence in 1921 and 1929

Nazi anti-Semitism in 1930s contributed to:
- increased Jewish immigration to Palestine
- Arab Rebellion 1936–9 and its suppression by British authorities
- British recommendation to partition Palestine 1937

Approach of Second World War led British to abandon partition and restrict Jewish immigration

2 The Birth of Israel 1939–49

POINTS TO CONSIDER

The Jews in Palestine largely supported the British during the Second World War. Then, when it ended, they went on the offensive in order to end British rule in Palestine and achieve a state of their own. When the British finally left Palestine in 1948, the neighbouring Arab states invaded the new state of Israel. These developments are examined under the headings:

- Terrorism and the end of British rule
- Partition and civil war 1947–8
- The war of 1948–9

The chapter then goes on to consider, in the key debate, how Israel won the war.

Key dates

1942		Biltmore Declaration of support for a 'Jewish commonwealth' in all of Palestine
1945		Zionist conference decided on a policy of active opposition to British rule
1946		Attack on the King David Hotel in Jerusalem
1947		Hanging of two British soldiers by Irgun
		The Exodus prevented from landing in Palestine
1947	November	United Nations vote for partition of Palestine
	November	Start of civil war in Palestine
	December	British announcement that they would leave Palestine
1948	May 14	British withdrawal from Palestine
	May 14	Declaration of new state of Israel
	May 15	Invasion of Israel by Arab armies
1949	January	Final ceasefire arranged

1 | Terrorism and the End of British Rule

Zionist policy in Palestine before the Second World War

The Jews in Palestine were represented by the **Jewish Agency**. This was effectively the government of the Jewish population in Palestine. It shaped Zionist policy in Palestine: for instance, it made decisions about Jewish settlements and the education of Jewish children. In 1937, the Jewish Agency had agreed to the British plan to divide Palestine into separate Jewish and Arab states. But even then, many Palestinian Jews foresaw that they would have to fight to defend a Jewish state. They knew that the Arabs would never agree to it. Furthermore, some Jewish leaders wanted *all* Palestine to be made into a Jewish state.

One of these was David Ben-Gurion, the leader of the Jewish Agency. He accepted the 1937 plan for the partition of Palestine with independent Jewish and Arab states. But he always hoped for more: he assumed that an independent state would allow for unlimited Jewish immigration, the development of a strong economy and the organisation of a powerful army. Then, after that, as he said in a letter to his son:

> I am certain we will be able to settle in all the other parts of the country, whether through agreement and mutual understanding with our Arab neighbours or in another way.

So, although the official policy of the Jewish Agency was to accept a Jewish state in *part* of Palestine, alongside an Arab one, Ben-Gurion and some other leaders hoped for a Jewish state in *all* of Palestine.

In 1939, the British decided *not* to partition Palestine (see page 14). This was a setback to Jewish hopes for a separate Jewish state but the Zionists were not about to give in. They began to campaign against the British policy. Then came the outbreak of the Second World War and most Palestinian Jews decided to support Britain in the fight against Nazi Germany. Many fought in the British army which, in the long term, would enable them to gain valuable military experience and, even, weapons. This would serve them well when the state of Israel was created.

From 1939 onwards, the British were preoccupied with winning the war against Germany. They gave little thought to the future of Palestine and maintained their policy of controlling Jewish immigration so as not to antagonise the Arabs. Then, in 1944, towards the end of the war, a British government committee discussed partition again only to abandon the idea after Lord Moyne, a government minister, was murdered by the **Stern gang**, a Jewish terrorist organisation.

British and Zionist policy after the Second World War

During the war the official Jewish policy in Palestine was to support the British war effort while continuing to campaign

Key question
What was Zionist policy in Palestine in the late 1930s?

Key terms

Jewish Agency
The governing body of the Zionist movement in Palestine during the British mandate.

Stern gang
A Zionist terrorist group founded in 1939.

Key question
How did Zionist policy change after the war?

Zionist conference decided on a policy of active opposition to British rule: 1945

Biltmore Declaration of support for a 'Jewish commonwealth' in all of Palestine: 1942

against the White Paper policy of 1939 that had opposed the idea of a separate Jewish state and sought to control immigration (see page 14). When the war ended in 1945 the British announced that there would be no change in their policy in Palestine: that is, there would be no big increase in immigration and no separate Jewish state. But the war had toughened the Zionists: six million Jews had been killed in the Nazi Holocaust and the Zionists were not in a mood to be patient. They were convinced that they had justice on their side and that international public opinion was coming round to support the idea of an independent Jewish state. In August 1945, the Zionist conference decided on a policy of active opposition to British rule in Palestine. Their leaders ordered the Haganah, the Jewish defence force, to co-operate with the **Irgun** and Stern gangs, two secret, underground Jewish organisations. British military bases, railways, trains and bridges in Palestine became the target of these terrorist groups.

US support for a Jewish state

Key question
Why was US support so important for the Zionists?

Irgun
A small secret Zionist organisation which fought for a Jewish state in all of Palestine.

Lobbied
To lobby is to win the support of members of a law-making body (e.g. the US Congress) so as to shape its policy.

The Zionists also decided that the USA, not Britain, was now the country they needed to have on their side. Only the USA, one of the two superpowers that emerged after the war, could put enough pressure on Britain to agree to a separate Jewish state and leave Palestine. The Zionists had the support of the Jewish population in the USA who could, in turn, put pressure on US government. There were four and a half million Jewish Americans, two million of them in New York city alone. By the end of the war, nearly all of them were Zionists, convinced of the need to establish an independent Jewish state for the Jewish refugees who had survived the Nazi Holocaust in Europe.

As early as May 1942, when news was only just beginning to emerge of the Nazi extermination of the Jews, the American Zionist conference had declared their support for a 'Jewish commonwealth' in *all* of Palestine. This became known as the Biltmore Declaration after the name of the hotel in New York in which the conference was held.

After the war, American Zionists, often joined by Jewish leaders from Palestine, launched a propaganda offensive: they addressed meetings, held rallies, placed advertisements and, above all, **lobbied** members of the US government and Congress, in order to win support. In April 1946, the US President, Harry Truman, called on the British government to allow the immediate entry of 100,000 Jewish refugees to Palestine. Six months later, he came out in support of the partition of Palestine.

Jewish terrorism

Key question
Why and how did the Zionists resort to terrorism in Palestine?

Meanwhile, in Palestine itself, the Zionists targeted the British. The reasons are not hard to see. The British authorities stopped boatloads of illegal Jewish immigrants from landing in Palestine. The British knew that Jewish immigration angered the Arabs and, when violence broke out between Jews and Arabs, British troops and police had to keep order. The British realised that further Jewish immigration would be resisted by the Arabs and lead to civil war so they refused to agree to any increase in immigration. The Haganah, for their part, did all they could to obstruct the British and to assist illegal immigration.

The Palestinian Arabs continued to oppose the idea of a Jewish state in Palestine. They feared that such a state would be filled by immigrants from Nazi Europe who would demand further expansion and a larger Jewish state incorporating all of Palestine. Besides, the Arabs felt that the West should take responsibility for the victims of the Holocaust. After all, the Holocaust had been carried out in the West. The Arabs felt that the Western powers should find a home for the Jews in another part of the world.

Bombing of British military headquarters in Jerusalem 1946

Jewish attacks on British forces now increased, sometimes in retaliation for death sentences passed on Jewish terrorists. In April 1946, six British soldiers were murdered in one incident and, in July 1946, the Irgun carried out their most spectacular act of terrorism – the attack on the King David Hotel in Jerusalem. This hotel housed the British military headquarters in Palestine. It was protected by barbed wire, machine guns and patrolling soldiers. At noon on 22 July 1946, a lorry drove up to the entrance of the hotel kitchen. Men dressed as Arabs got out and unloaded their cargo of milk churns. They rolled them into the building. No one guessed that the milk churns contained high explosives or that the 'Arabs' were members of Irgun. At 12.37pm the explosion tore through the building killing 88 people, including 15 Jews.

Other terrorist acts

Terrorist incidents like these weakened the morale of the British, both in Palestine and at home. They also led to frustration and anger at what the British saw as support for terrorism from American Zionists. After the killing of 20 British soldiers in the officers' club in Jerusalem in February 1947, the British Prime Minister complained of a report he had heard that the Mayor of New York had launched a Zionist drive to raise £2 million for the purchase of 'men, guns and money'. The British leader protested that:

> the guns which are being subscribed for in America can only be required to shoot at British soldiers in Palestine.

In the summer of 1947 two incidents finally convinced the British that they should withdraw from Palestine. One was the hanging of two British soldiers in revenge for the execution of three Irgun members: a photograph of the two men hanging from a tree appeared on the front page of several British newspapers. The other incident involved a ship called *The Exodus* which was carrying 4500 refugees from Europe. It was prevented, by the British authorities, from landing its passengers in Palestine and was sent back to Europe. This incident attracted widespread

Key dates

Attack on the King David Hotel in Jerusalem: 1946

Hanging of two British soldiers by Irgun: 1947

The Exodus prevented from landing in Palestine: 1947

This photograph appeared on the front page of the *Daily Express* in August 1947. It shows two British soldiers who had been hanged by members of Irgun. What impact would this have on British public opinion?

publicity, winning much sympathy for the Jewish refugees, and was thus a huge propaganda success for the Zionists. As a result of actions like these, the British authorities came in for worldwide criticism.

The British were also exhausted after the war, with food shortages and rationing at home, and could hardly afford to keep 100,000 troops and police in Palestine. After 30 years of trying to solve the problems of Palestine, the British government decided that it would hand it over to the United Nations (UN) in May 1948.

Summary diagram: Terrorism and the end of British rule

Official Jewish policy in Palestine

Before the war	**During the war**	**After the war**
accepted partition, then campaigned against the White Paper 1939	supported the British and gained military experience	used propaganda (especially in the USA) to gain support for a Jewish state and used terrorism to drive out the British

2 | Partition and Civil War 1947–8

UN vote for partition, November 1947

As early as February 1947 the British government sought the advice of the UN which had been formed at the end of the Second World War. The UN Special Committee on Palestine (UNSCOP) was set up to investigate, and then make recommendations on how to resolve, the Palestine problem. The UNSCOP report was completed in August and, three months later, in November, the **UN General Assembly** voted to accept its recommendations. The main recommendation was to divide Palestine and set up both a Jewish and an Arab state. The areas that were more Jewish (in population and land ownership) were to be allocated to the Jewish state and those which were mainly Arab to the Arab state. As you can see on the map below, this resulted in a criss-cross arrangement with 'kissing points' at the intersections. The UN thought that this would force the two sides to co-operate! The holy city of Jerusalem was to be an international zone governed by an international force.

Key question
What was the response to the UNSCOP report?

Key date
United Nations vote for partition of Palestine: November 1947

Key term
UN General Assembly
The main body of the UN in which every state is represented.

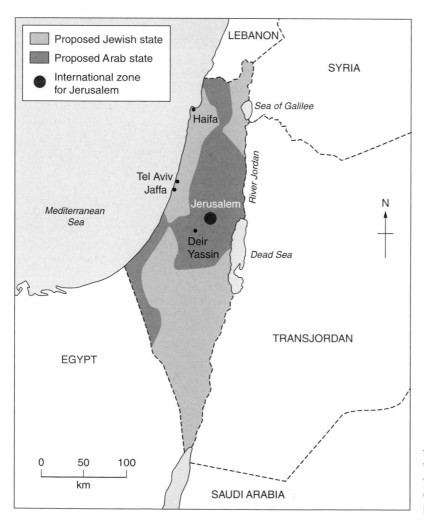

The UN partition plan. What problems might you expect in a state divided into three parts?

The Jewish Agency in Palestine officially accepted the plan despite the exclusion of Jerusalem from the Jewish state: the Jews in Palestine were pleased that they now had international support for the idea of a Jewish state. But not all of them were happy with the plan: not only was Jerusalem excluded from the Jewish state but many Jewish settlements were to be included in the Arab state. Menachem Begin, leader of Irgun, announced:

> The partition of the homeland is illegal. It will never be recognised. It will not bind the Jewish people. Jerusalem was and will forever be our capital. **Eretz Israel** will be restored to the people of Israel. All of it. And for ever.

David Ben-Gurion said:

> Tens of thousands of our youth are prepared to lay down their lives for the sake of Jerusalem. It is within the boundaries of the state of Israel just as Tel Aviv is.

The **Arab Higher Committee**, representing the Palestinian Arabs, rejected the UN partition plan, especially as the Jews were to be given the larger area. The Arabs did not wish to give up any of their land. They felt that the Western powers should find a home for the Jews elsewhere.

Civil war in Palestine, November 1947 to May 1948

A few days after the UN voted for partition, the Arab Higher Committee proclaimed a three-day strike which led to outbreaks of violence against Jewish civilians. However, the Jewish Agency and its forces were ready to respond. They had always known that the Arabs would resist the establishment of a Jewish state in Palestine. In December, when the British announced that they would leave Palestine in May 1948, the fighting between Arabs and Jews intensified. At first, the Jewish forces acted defensively: they sought to hold on to and defend the land they had been allocated by the UN. However, they soon also went on the offensive and fought to gain control of Jewish settlements in the land allocated to the Arabs and of the roads leading to them.

In 1948, soldiers from Syria and Iraq began to cross into Palestine to help the Arabs. Again, this was no surprise to the Jewish leaders. They fully expected neighbouring Arab states to invade Palestine when the British left and the new Jewish state came into existence. So they resolved to secure control over Jewish territory. In March the Haganah came up with Plan D, the aim of which was to:

- take over any installations evacuated by the British, especially military bases
- expel as many Palestinians as possible from the future Jewish state.

Key terms

Eretz Israel
The Land of Israel, as in the Bible. In effect, this meant the whole of Palestine, not just the area allocated to the Jewish state by the UN.

Arab Higher Committee
A committee of Palestinian Arab leaders.

Key question
Why was there a civil war in Palestine?

Key dates

Start of civil war in Palestine: November 1947

British announcement that they would leave Palestine: December 1947

Already, by February 1948, many of the Palestinian élite, such as landowners and business people, had left Palestine. This contributed to feelings of insecurity among the Arab masses, especially in the villages, and encouraged others to leave. Then, in April 1948, Jewish forces began the forcible expulsion of Arabs from villages inside what was to become the Jewish state. Nearly all of the villages along the coast from Tel Aviv to Haifa (see the map on page 20) were cleared of their Arab populations. Armed Jewish forces surrounded each village on three sides, forcing the villagers to flee through the fourth side. If the people refused to leave, they were often forced on to lorries and driven away to Transjordan. Similarly, Jewish forces took over mixed Arab–Jewish towns like Jaffa and Haifa. In Haifa, where explosions were set off by Jewish forces in Arab areas of the city, nearly all of the Arab population of 100,000 fled.

The battle for Jerusalem

There was a particularly bitter struggle to control the roads leading to Jerusalem and massacres of civilians were carried out by both sides. Some of the massacres by Jewish forces were in retaliation for Palestinian attacks on Jewish settlements or on convoys trying to supply the Jewish population of Jerusalem. However, the targets for Jewish attacks were not random: they were carefully chosen. They were intended to rid the future Jewish state of as many Arabs as possible. In the weeks before the British withdrawal from Palestine, some of the bloodiest fighting took place in and around Jerusalem. In one well-known incident, in April 1948, Irgun fighters, led by Menachem Begin, attacked the village of Deir Yassin (which was inside what was to be Arab territory under the UN plan) and killed the inhabitants. They said they believed it was an Arab headquarters. The effects of incidents like this were dramatic. As Begin himself wrote later:

British withdrawal from Palestine: 14 May 1948

Key date

> The Arabs began to flee in terror even before they clashed with Jewish forces. … Arab propaganda spread a legend of terror amongst Arabs and Arab troops, who were seized with panic at the mention of Irgun soldiers. The legend was worth half a dozen battalions to the forces of Israel.

By 14 May 1948, when the British finally withdrew from Palestine, over 300,000 Arabs had left what was to become the new Jewish state. This was a victory for the Jews but a disaster for the Arabs.

Summary diagram: Partition and civil war 1947–8

Partition and civil war

November 1947 UN voted to partition Palestine	Civil war, November 1947–May 1948
• official Zionist policy to accept partition, although some wanted all of Palestine for Jewish state • Palestinian Arabs rejected partition	• massacres committed by both Arabs and Jews • Jewish forces expelled Arabs from land allocated to state of Israel

3 | The War of 1948–9

Key dates

Declaration of new state of Israel: 14 May 1948

Invasion of Israel by Arab armies: 15 May 1948

On the 14 May 1948 David Ben-Gurion proclaimed the birth of the new state of Israel. The next day armed forces from Lebanon, Syria, Iraq, Transjordan and Egypt invaded. The state of Israel was thus born in war and its first aim was survival. Israel's War of Independence was to consist of three phases of fighting, interspersed by UN ceasefires.

The first phase of fighting, 15 May to 10 June 1948

In the south an Egyptian army of 10,000 men crossed the border near the coast and attacked some isolated Jewish settlements in what was to be the Arab state. In the north, Syrian, Iraqi and Lebanese troops crossed the border but were resisted by Jewish settlers and most of the invaders were forced to withdraw. They lacked ammunition and were the least experienced of the Arab forces.

Key question
Why was the struggle for Jerusalem so important for the Israelis?

The major conflict was the battle for Jerusalem, just as it had been in the final days of the British mandate. King Abdullah of Transjordan moved his **Arab Legion** to defend the Old City, the eastern part, of Jerusalem. His army was the one that the Israelis were keenest to defeat, for two main reasons. First, they wanted to gain control of all of the city of Jerusalem, including the Old City which contained the Jewish holy places. Secondly, they knew that the Legion was the most effective and best-trained Arab army and they believed that, if they could defeat it, then the other Arab armies would collapse. However, the Israelis were not able to defeat the Legion and the Israeli offensive was halted. Nevertheless, the Israelis did gain control of west Jerusalem without a big struggle and were thus able to feed and protect the Jewish population in that part of the city.

Key term

Arab Legion
The army of Transjordan.

Ceasefire, June 1948

On 10 June the UN persuaded the warring parties to agree to a ceasefire. The Jordanians and Lebanese were willing to open peace talks but the Egyptians, Syrians and Iraqis were not. During the lull, the Israelis secured fresh supplies of weapons from Eastern Europe, mainly from the Czechs. (Britain had been the main supplier of arms to Egypt, Jordan and Iraq but was unwilling to disobey the UN embargo on supplying arms to the warring sides.) The Israelis used the ceasefire to recruit and retrain more men as well as to reorganise and re-arm their forces. This gave them a significant advantage and, when the Egyptians broke the truce, the Israelis went on the offensive and seized the initiative from the Arab forces.

The second phase of fighting, 9–18 July 1948

In the second phase of fighting, the Israeli priority was to try to widen the corridor leading to Jerusalem, taking land allocated to the Arabs in the process. They were particularly keen to control this territory in order to forestall any UN peace plan that might force them back to the borders which had been drawn in the 1947 partition plan. They were largely successful but the Arab Legion held the Old City of Jerusalem. What the Arab Legion did not attempt was to seize land allocated to the Jewish state. In the south, the Israelis resisted further Egyptian advances in the Negev (see the map on page 25) while, in the north, they gained control of the whole Galilee region, including land that had been allocated to the Arabs. In the 10 days of fighting in this second phase of the war, Israel improved its position and was to retain the initiative for the rest of the war.

In September, during the second truce, the special UN mediator, Count Bernadotte from Sweden, came up with a peace plan: it gave added land to the Arabs in the south and more land to the Israelis in the north but Jerusalem was still to be an international city, under UN control, and the Arab refugees were all to have the right to return home. The next day Bernadotte was assassinated by the Stern gang. The new Israeli government was keen to maintain international support and ordered the dissolution of the Stern gang and Irgun. Some of their members were then incorporated into the **Israeli Defence Force (IDF)**.

Israeli Defence Force (IDF)
The Israeli armed forces, most of whose members had been in the Haganah.

Key term

The third phase of fighting, 15 October 1948 to 7 January 1949

In mid-October, Israel broke the second ceasefire and concentrated on defeating the Egyptians in the south. This they did, even pursuing the Egyptian army over the border into Egypt. They agreed, under American pressure, to withdraw from Egyptian territory but they remained in complete control of the Negev when the final ceasefire was arranged in January 1949.

Final ceasefire arranged: January 1949

Key date

The results of the war

Israel emerged from the war exhausted but well organised. The new nation had lost 6000 lives, which amounted to one per cent of the entire Jewish population of 650,000. However, the Israelis now controlled 79 per cent of what had been the British mandate of Palestine rather than the 55 per cent allocated to the new state by the UN (see the map on page 25). By the end of the war, over

Key question
Who won and who lost in the war?

Israeli gains in the
1948–9 war.

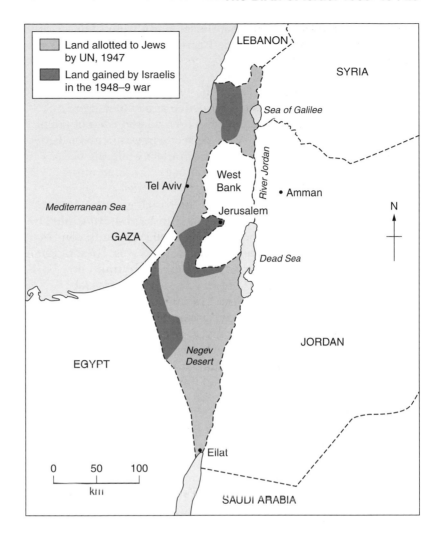

700,000 Palestinian Arabs had become refugees, having fled or
been driven from their homes. Most ended up in Gaza or what
became known as the West Bank (see the map above). This flight,
and the events of 1947–49 as a whole, have become known in
Arabic as the '*Nakbah*', the catastrophe or disaster.

For the Israelis, this had been the war of national liberation.
They had survived their first great test and were confident of
their future as an independent nation. An American Zionist,
Nahum Goldmann, wrote of the psychological effects of the
Israeli victory:

> It seemed to show the advantages of direct action over negotiation
> and diplomacy. ... The victory offered such a glorious contrast to
> the centuries of persecution and humiliation, of adaptation and
> compromise, that it seemed to indicate the only direction that
> could possibly be taken from then on. To tolerate no attack ... and
> shape history by creating facts so simple, so compelling, so
> satisfying that it became Israel's policy in its conflict with the Arab
> world.

Key term

Nakbah
An Arabic word for
'catastrophe' or
'disaster', used to
refer to the 1948–9
war and the
creation of the
Palestinian refugee
problem.

What, according to the writer, had Israel learnt from their victory in the war? How was this to shape Israel's policy towards the Arabs?

Armistice agreements

Between January and July 1949 **armistice** agreements were signed, under UN supervision, between Israel and each of the neighbouring Arab states. The first agreement was between Israel and Egypt. It confirmed their pre-war borders while the Gaza area of Arab Palestine (see the map on page 25) came under Egyptian military rule.

King Abdullah of Transjordan and the Israeli government were keen to reach agreement with each other and did so in April. The King wanted his forces to keep control of the West Bank, the name given to the Palestinian Arab land on the west bank of the river Jordan (see the map on page 25). This area would now be governed as part of his kingdom. In this way, most of Arab Palestine, including the Old City of Jerusalem, now became part of the new, enlarged Kingdom of Jordan as the state became known. The Israelis were keen to make peace with the King so that they could keep control of the newer, western part of Jerusalem. They preferred a partitioned Jerusalem to the international zone that the USA and the UN wanted.

Reaching agreement between Israel and Syria took longer. When the fighting in the north had ended, Syrian forces were in control of some territory that had been allocated to the new Jewish state. In July 1948, the UN negotiated that the Syrians would withdraw from the ceasefire lines if the vacated area became a demilitarised zone. This meant that Israel could not station any troops or weapons there. This agreement left Israel free of Syrian troops on its territory while providing a buffer zone between the two sides.

The elusive peace

The armistice agreements were supposed to lead to permanent peace treaties but there was to be no such treaty between Israel and an Arab nation for nearly 30 years. The two key issues on which no agreement could be reached were borders and refugees.

Some Arab states were willing to negotiate over borders but all of them stuck to the policy formulated by the **Arab League** on refugees: that Israel had created the problem and the refugees had the 'right to return' to their homes or to be compensated by Israel. The Israelis, for their part, claimed that the Arabs had created the refugee problem by invading Israel and starting the war. The Israelis would only negotiate if it was agreed that most of the refugees should be settled *outside* Israel.

There were further obstacles to permanent peace. First, public opinion in the Arab countries was intensely bitter over their defeat and in their hatred of Israel. Secondly, for the Israeli government, peace with its Arab neighbours was desirable but it was not worth the price of giving up any territory or agreeing to the return of large numbers of Palestinian refugees. Besides, the

Key question
What was agreed under the armistices?

Key question
Why was there no peace treaty?

Key terms

Armistice
An agreement to stop fighting.

Arab League
A body established in 1945 to represent the Arab states.

Israelis believed that time was on their side: the UN would get used to the new, expanded borders of the Israeli state and to the idea of a divided Jerusalem rather than push for the international control that they had originally envisaged for the city in the plan of 1947. In other words, Israel decided that it did not need permanent peace with the Arabs or a solution to the Palestinian refugee problem. Its priorities were now to build the new state, implement large-scale Jewish immigration and consolidate their independence.

Summary diagram: The war of 1948–9

First phase of war, May–June 1948
- Israelis resisted invasion from north
- failed to defeat Arab Legion but gained control of west Jerusalem

Second phase of war, July 1948
- Israelis re-equipped and reorganised during ceasefire
- Israelis gained land in north and kept control of west Jerusalem

Third phase of war, October 1948 to January 1949
- Israelis defeated Egyptians

Results of war
- Israeli victory secured survival of new state and gained more land
- 700,000 Palestinian Arabs became refugees before and during the war
- *Nakbah*, or catastrophe, for Palestinians
- Armistices agreed but no peace treaty
- Jordan took control of West Bank
- Egypt took control of Gaza

4 | The Key Debate: How did Israel Win the War?

There is wide variation in how historians explain the outcome of the first Arab–Israeli war. The Zionist interpretation goes like this: the war was a struggle between tiny Israel and a huge Arab **coalition** made up of several armies. Israel was fighting for its own survival against Arab forces that were united in their aim of destroying the new state. Israel was the tiny David fighting against a massive Arab Goliath. Furthermore, Israel had far fewer weapons yet, against all the odds, it won the war through the heroic efforts, tenacity and courage of its people. This is the popular, heroic interpretation, which is still largely taught in Israeli schools today. It is mostly based on fact but on selectively chosen facts.

In the past 20 years historians have gained access to and analysed Israeli government documents from the time of the war. Several Israeli historians, such as Avi Shlaim and Benny Morris, have produced a new, **revisionist** interpretation of how Israel won. This new, revisionist history focuses on two main areas: on

Key terms

Coalition
A union of two or more groups for a specific purpose.

Revisionist
A 'revised' interpretation based on a critical re-examination of historical facts.

the military balance between the two sides and on the war aims of the Arabs.

The military balance

The Zionist version of history maintains that the Arab forces always had far larger numbers of troops and of weapons. It is certainly true that, at the start of the war, the Israelis only had about 30,000 soldiers and that their weapons were inferior. But they built up the army to about 65,000 by July and had nearly 100,000 in arms by December 1948. The total number of Arab troops involved in the fighting was similar at the start and was also built up during the war but not as fast as that of the Israelis. With regard to weaponry, the Israelis were poorly equipped at the start but, particularly during the first truce in June–July 1948, they gained access to much more equipment from Europe and thus were better armed for the rest of the war. In short, the stronger side won.

The Israelis also had other military advantages. About 25,000 Israelis had fought in the British army in the Second World War and gained valuable experience in training, organisation and technology. The only Arab force that was as well trained and disciplined was the 10,000 of the Arab Legion of Transjordan (which was partly financed by Britain and was led by British officers).

Key question
Which side had the stronger military forces?

War aims

The Jews in Palestine, particularly under the leadership of Ben-Gurion, had recognised, for several years, that they would need to use force to establish their new state. In this, they were united. The Palestinian Arabs, on the other hand, lacked strong, united leadership. They were let down by their leaders, many of whom had left Palestine in the final days of the British mandate. The governments of the neighbouring Arab states had begun to plan for invasion only in April 1948. They had agreed on a plan and King Abdullah of Transjordan claimed to be commander-in-chief. But the Arab leaders were not united in their goals and each tended to fight for their own particular interests, which often meant to gain control of a piece of Palestinian territory for themselves. There was very little co-ordination of their efforts in the war and both the Egyptian and Syrian governments were deeply suspicious of King Abdullah's aims.

King Abdullah and the Israelis

The case of King Abdullah of Transjordan is particularly significant. Before the war he had held a secret meeting with one of the Israeli leaders. He had let it be known that he did not think the Palestinian Arab state could survive on its own. He thought it would be too weak and he wished to attach it to his state. He saw himself as the leader of an enlarged Arab state (and, in this, he had some support from the British). He also led Jewish leaders to believe that he would *not* invade territory allocated to

Key question
What were the war aims of King Abdullah of Jordan?

the new Jewish state. No actual agreements were made at this meeting but a mutual understanding was established.

When the war started, Abdullah's Arab Legion advanced to defend the Old City, the eastern part of Jerusalem, against the Israeli offensive and they held on to it throughout the war. Yet the Arab Legion made little effort to stop the Israelis seizing west Jerusalem. Nor did the Legion invade the territory of the new Jewish state. Furthermore, the Arab Legion remained neutral when the Israelis fought Egyptian forces and did not join in support of Egyptian forces in the second and third phases of the war.

In other words, the army from Transjordan invaded what was to be the new Arab state but it never invaded Jewish, Israeli territory. Its aim was to gain control of most of Arab Palestine (on the western side of the river Jordan), which it did, but not to destroy the state of Israel. Israel was able to exploit its understanding with Transjordan in order to break the chain of hostile Arab states, deepen the divisions in the Arab coalition and pick off its Arab opponents one by one. The fact that Israel and Transjordan were 'the best of enemies' is largely ignored in the heroic interpretation of the war which sees the little Israeli David pitted against the united Arab world of Goliath.

Some key books in the debate

Chaim Herzog, *The Arab–Israeli Wars* (Arms and Armour Press, 1982), offers a Zionist interpretation.

Benny Morris, *1948: The First Arab–Israeli War* (Yale University Press, 2008), offers a revisionist interpretation.

Avi Shlaim, *The Iron Wall – Israel and the Arab World* (Penguin, 2001), offers another revisionist interpretation.

Study Guide

In the style of Edexcel and OCR

To what extent was the West responsible for the creation of the state of Israel?

Exam tips

The cross-references are intended to take you straight to the material that will help you to answer the question.

First, re-read pages 5–14 and 16–21.

To answer this question you need to analyse Western policy towards Palestine/Israel, then other factors that contributed to the creation of the new state and, finally, make a judgement about the relative importance of Western policy in comparison to other factors.

You could examine Western involvement through:

- the Balfour Declaration
- the League of Nations mandate
- British rule in Palestine before the Second World War, e.g. in allowing Jewish immigration and in suppressing the Arab Rebellion after 1936
- US, and wider, international support for the creation of the state of Israel after 1945.

You then need to examine other factors, especially the active part played by Jews in Palestine and abroad, for example:

- maintaining British support up to 1945 (for instance, by serving in the British army)
- use of force by Jews in Palestine to end British rule after 1945
- gaining sympathy and exploiting support (e.g. through propaganda) as a result of the Holocaust
- developing US (and, later, UN) support for a Jewish state during and after the Second World War.

Finally, you will need to arrive at a conclusion which weighs up the importance of Western policy against these other factors. Do this briefly but very clearly, highlighting one or two key points rather than repeating much of what you have said before.

In the style of the International Baccalaureate

Source A

Extract from the report of the UN Special Committee on Palestine (UNSCOP), August 1947.

The basic conflict in Palestine is a clash of two intense nationalisms ... there are now in Palestine some 650,000 Jews and 1,200,000 Arabs who are dissimilar in their ways of living and, for the time being, separated by political interests which render difficult full and effective political co-operation. ... It is recognised that partition has been strongly opposed by Arabs, but it is felt that opposition would be lessened by a solution which definitively fixes the extent of territory to be allotted to the Jews with its implicit limitation on immigration. The fact that the solution carries the sanction of the United Nations involves a finality which should allay Arab fears of further expansion of the Jewish state.

Source B

A cartoon from the *Daily Mail* in September 1947. The figure on the right represents a Jew and on the left an Arab.

Source C

The Palestinian Arab response to the UNSCOP proposals for partition was conveyed to the UN by Jamal al-Husseini, the leader of the Arab Higher Committee, September 1947.

The Zionists claimed the establishment of a Jewish national home by virtue of the Balfour Declaration. But the British government had no right to dispose of Palestine which it had occupied in the name of the Allies as a liberator and not a conqueror. The Balfour Declaration was in contradiction with the Covenant of the League of Nations and was an immoral, unjust and illegal promise.

The solution lay in the Charter of the United Nations, in accordance with which the Arabs of Palestine, who constituted the majority, were entitled to a free and independent state. ... Once Palestine was found to be entitled to independence, the United Nations was not legally competent to decide or impose the constitutional organisation of Palestine, since such action would amount to interference with an internal matter of an independent nation.

Source D

Palestinian Jewish views of the UNSCOP proposals for partition were conveyed to the UN by Rabbi Hillel Silver of the Jewish Agency for Palestine, October 1947.

The plan proposed that the city of Jerusalem should be established as a separate unit. But modern Jerusalem contained a compact Jewish community of 90,000 inhabitants, and included the central national, religious and educational institutions of the Jewish people of Palestine. ... It was the ancient capital of the Jewish nation and its symbol throughout the ages. ... If that heavy sacrifice was the inescapable condition of a final solution ... then the Jewish Agency was prepared to recommend the acceptance of the partition solution ... subject to further discussion of constitutional and territorial provisions.

Source E

Extract from: A History of Modern Palestine, *2004, by Ilan Pappe, a 'revisionist' Israeli historian.*

The Palestinian refusal to accept a UN solution provided a pretext [excuse or given reason] for implementing a systematic expulsion of the local population within the areas allocated for a Jewish state, areas already demarcated in the UNSCOP report. ... Twelve days after the adoption of the UN resolution [in November 1947], the expulsion of Palestinians began. A month later, the first Palestinian village was wiped out by Jewish retaliation to a Palestinian attack on convoys and Jewish settlements. This action was transformed into an ethnic cleansing operation in March, which resulted in the loss to Palestine of much of its indigenous [original] population.

(a) (i) What, according to Source A, might lessen Arab opposition to partition? (2 marks)
    (ii) What is the message of Source D? (3 marks)
(b) In what ways does the message of Source B support the views expressed in Source A? (6 marks)
(c) With reference to their origin and purpose, assess the value and limitations of Sources C and E for historians studying the origins of the Israeli–Palestinian conflict. (6 marks)
(d) Using these sources and your own knowledge, explain to what extent you agree with the view that it was the Palestinian Arab refusal to accept the UN partition plan that led to increased conflict in Palestine. (8 marks)

Exam tips
The cross-references are intended to take you straight to the material that will help you to answer the questions.

Re-read pages 16–22.

(a) (i) Source A suggests that a fixed limit to the territory allotted to the Jews might lessen Arab opposition as it implies a limit to the amount of immigration. Also, the fact that it is a UN solution suggests that it is final.

(ii) To answer this question, first explain what the UNSCOP proposal for Jerusalem was. Then explain why it caused such concern. On what conditions might the Jewish Agency recommend acceptance of the plan?

(b) First, you need to explain the message of Source B. What does the cartoonist think will happen when the British mandate is ended? Does your interpretation of the cartoon support the view, in Source A, of two competing national groups with opposing political interests? Is there any similarity in the cartoonist's view of Britain's role and the effect that partition, in UNSCOP's view, might have?

(c) Source C: explain who the author was and how representative of Arab opinion you think he was. Explain why he focuses on the Balfour Declaration. How, in his opinion, should the UN have acted over Palestine? What had the UN done wrong? What light do these views throw on actions taken by the Arabs in the months ahead?

Source E: what is the value, and what are the limitations, of a historian's view? And, specifically, of an Israeli and a 'revisionist' historian? (For definition of 'revisionist' see the glossary.) What is his main point? How does this add to our understanding of the origins of the Arab–Jewish conflict?

(d) Sources A, C and E all provide some support, even if indirectly, for the view that it was the Palestinian Arab refusal to accept the UN partition plan that led to increased conflict.

- Source A recognises that conflict originated in the clash of two 'nationalisms' but that it was the Arabs who opposed partition. It also believes, rather optimistically, that a UN solution might lessen the opposition and, by implication, the danger of conflict.
- Source C shows that the Arabs believed that the Balfour Declaration and the UN partition plan were both illegal, i.e. that Britain and the UN bear responsibility for the conflict. You should, however, explain how this view might suggest a reason for refusing to accept the plan.
- Source E: for what, according to the author, does the Palestinian Arab refusal provide a pretext? Does his view suggest that it was primarily the Arabs who were responsible for increased conflict? Your own knowledge will be particularly useful here, e.g. about the fighting within the territory to be allotted to the Jews (pages 21–2).

- Source B suggests neither Arab nor Jew is more to blame while showing that the conflict is bottled up, or at least contained, by the cork provided by the British mandate. Might it also suggest that the British departure would lead to escalation of the conflict?
- Source D: what is the Jews' main concern about the partition plan? Would the Jews, nevertheless, accept the plan? If so, without reservations? Again, your wider knowledge could and should be brought in here, e.g. about the fighting over the roads to Jerusalem, Deir Yassin, etc. (page 22).

Your own knowledge should inform your judgement about what can be learnt from the sources and you might make some reference to increasing Jewish immigration (especially as a result of the Nazi Holocaust) and British, and later US, policy in leading to the conflict, and the need for UN intervention, in the first place.

In concluding, you need to make a judgement about the extent to which it was the Arab refusal to accept the plan that led to increased conflict.

3 Arab–Israeli Wars in 1956, 1967 and 1973

POINTS TO CONSIDER

When the state of Israel was created in 1948 it was immediately plunged into war with the surrounding Arab states. The new state survived its first war but, over the next 25 years, there were to be three more major conflicts between Israel and its Arab neighbours. This chapter examines the causes and consequences of each of those wars. Then, finally, it recounts how Egypt became the first Arab state to sign a peace treaty with Israel. These events are considered under the following headings:

- Egypt and the Suez crisis
- The Suez War 1956
- The causes of the Six-Day War 1967
- The Six-Day War and its results
- From war to peace: Yom Kippur to Camp David 1973–8

Key dates

1949		First Arab–Israeli war ended in defeat for Arabs
1952		King of Egypt overthrown by army officers
1954		Nasser became President of Egypt
1955	February	Israeli attack on Gaza
	September	Egypt announced Czech arms deal
1956	July	Nationalisation of Suez Canal
	October 29	Israeli forces invaded Egypt
	October 31	British and French bombed Egyptian airfields
	November 6	UN ceasefire and Anglo-French withdrawal from Egypt
1964		Palestine Liberation Organisation (PLO) established
1965		Fatah carried out its first raid on Israel
1966		Egypt signed a defence agreement with Syria
1967	April 7	Air fight between Israeli and Syrian planes
	May 15	Nasser moved Egyptian troops into Sinai

	May 22	Nasser closed the Straits of Tiran to Israeli shipping
	May 30	Jordan signed a defence treaty with Egypt
	June 5–10	Six-Day War
	November	UN Resolution 242
1970		Anwar Sadat became President of Egypt
1973	October 6–24	Yom Kippur War
1978		Camp David Agreement between Egypt and Israel
1979		Treaty of Washington between Egypt and Israel
1981		Assassination of President Sadat

1 | Egypt and the Suez Crisis

Israel and its Arab neighbours

The Arab states were stung by their defeat against Israel in 1949. Their peoples felt bitter about their humiliation: it showed how weak and divided they were. It made them bitterly anti-Western. The Arabs felt that the USA had bullied the UN into creating the new state of Israel. They now suspected that the Western powers, such as Britain, France and the USA, would use Israel as a base from which to keep an eye on the Arab states. There was no peace treaty between Israel and any of the Arab states and the ceasefire lines continued to be a source of tension, sometimes fighting.

Israel and Syria

In 1949, the UN had persuaded Israel and Syria to agree to a demilitarised zone along their border. This zone was inside the territory of the new state of Israel and it contained many Arab villages. The Israelis tried to force the Arabs out of some these villages and develop Jewish settlements. The Syrians objected to this. There were frequent incidents of shelling by both sides. There were also disputes over Israel's attempts to divert the waters of the river Jordan in order to irrigate dry parts of the new state.

Israel and Jordan

There was similar tension along the border between Israel and what now became known as the state of Jordan (see the map on page 25). The latter was made up of what had been Transjordan together with the West Bank of the river Jordan now added to it. In 1951 King Abdullah was assassinated by a Muslim fanatic and, after a short reign by his unstable son, his grandson, Hussein, became King in 1953.

The expanded state of Jordan now included a million Palestinian Arabs who were granted full rights as citizens of Jordan. They included many who had fled from their homes in

Key question
What were the causes of tension on Israel's borders?

Key date

First Arab–Israeli war ended in defeat for Arabs: 1949

Reprisal
An act of retaliation against an enemy to stop them from doing something again.

Fedayeen
Men trained to carry out raids (literally, 'those who sacrifice themselves').

Imperialism
Rule by one nation or people over another.

what was now the state of Israel and who were determined to return. However, every time they crossed the border into Israel, there were Israeli **reprisals**. In their reprisals, the Israeli military forces usually targeted Arab villages which they suspected of helping the infiltrators. The government of Jordan tried to restrain the Palestinians from carrying out raids into Israel but the Israelis were not satisfied and, in October 1953, after an Israeli woman and her two children were killed, the Israeli forces attacked the Jordanian village of Qibya, blowing up 45 houses and killing more than 50 of the inhabitants, most of whom were women and children.

Israel and Egypt

Despite the ferocity of the Qibya reprisal raid, it was on Israel's border with Egypt that the most frequent killings occurred. There were 300,000 Palestinians in the narrow coastal area known as the Gaza Strip (see the map on page 25). At the end of the war in 1949, this area came under Egyptian military control. The majority of its inhabitants were refugees, forced to flee from their homes between 1947 and 1949. Many of them were set on returning to their homes, especially those who had left villages just across the border. There were frequent raids into Israel. Some of these were carried out by Palestinian fighters, or *fedayeen*, who attacked Israeli settlements, but the vast majority were by unarmed Palestinians. Often they wanted to visit relatives, reclaim their possessions, harvest their crops or just graze their animals on what was now Israeli land. However, as on the Jordanian border, the Israeli Defence Forces (IDF) retaliated with reprisal raids. These raids and reprisals intensified in the mid-1950s. To understand the reasons for this increased tension and the outbreak of a second Arab–Israeli war, we need to examine what happened in Egypt after the end of the 1948–9 war.

Egypt and the rise of Nasser

Along with millions of other Arabs, the Egyptians felt bitter about their defeat at the hands of the Israelis in 1947. Egypt was the largest Arab state and it had a long, proud history. It was also strategically important: it was the bridge between Africa and Asia. Even more importantly, the Suez Canal, which passed through its territory, was the main trading link between Europe and the East. It was a particularly vital link for Britain which had many military bases in the East and which depended on supplies of oil from the Persian Gulf (see the map on page 38).

The Suez Canal had been built by the French and British in the 1880s. Or rather, the British and French used Egyptian labour to build it and thousands of Egyptians died in its construction. Seventy years later, in the 1950s, it was still so important to the British that they had 70,000 troops stationed in the Canal zone. This was intolerable to many Egyptians. They saw it as an example of British **imperialism**. They felt they could only be truly independent once the British had left.

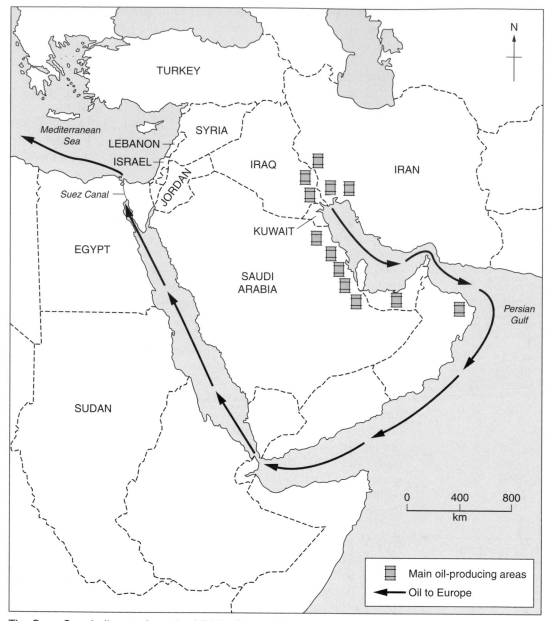

The Suez Canal oil route from the Middle East to Europe.

Many Egyptians blamed their government and, in particular, King Farouk for their country's weakness. They felt the King's government was manipulated by the British. Some Egyptians, especially in the army, blamed the government for their defeat by the Israelis in 1949. Many of the younger army officers accused the authorities of supplying them with poor equipment and incompetent commanders.

Nasser and the Egyptian revolution

Gamal Abdul Nasser was one of a number of young officers who came from a poor background but had received an education and risen up through the ranks of the army. A group of these young officers, who called themselves the Free Officers, secretly plotted to overthrow the government. They took their time, building up support within the army while avoiding being uncovered or captured by the security police. In July 1952, they struck. They took over the key government buildings and announced the success of the revolution over the radio. They allowed the King to flee the country. He had lost much respect, especially after divorcing his popular Egyptian wife and spending much of his time in expensive European resorts on the Mediterranean.

The head of the new government was General Neguib, one of the more respected of the senior army officers and, when Egypt became a republic in 1953, he became President. However, the most powerful member of the new government was Colonel Nasser. He had never forgotten the dying words of a comrade in the 1948–9 war: 'Remember the real battle is in Egypt.' He believed the first part of this battle had now been won with the removal of the King's government. The second part was to make his country truly independent and that meant freeing Egypt of foreign (i.e. British) troops.

In 1954 Nasser became president and, after long discussions, he persuaded the British to withdraw their troops from the Suez Canal zone. Britain, like the USA, still wished to keep on good terms with Nasser. They wanted Arab support in the Middle East against the **Soviet Union**. They wanted an alliance with Egypt as it was the strongest, most developed Arab nation and because the Suez Canal passed through its territory.

Colonel Nasser was one of the army officers who overthrew the unpopular royal government of Egypt in 1952. In 1954 he became President of Egypt.

The Israeli attack on Gaza, February 1955

However, Nasser wanted Egypt to be neutral and was not willing to join an anti-Soviet alliance. This worried the West. The Israelis were also worried, but for different reasons. They wanted to hit back at Egypt for encouraging Palestinian raids into Israel: they wanted to teach Nasser a lesson and, perhaps, remove him from power. The Israeli leader, Ben-Gurion, said to his cabinet:

> It is definitely possible to topple him and it is even a *mitzvah* [sacred obligation] to do so. Who is he anyway, this Nasser-Shmasser?

One way to undermine him was to show him up as militarily weak. This way he would be cut down to size, to a mere 'Nasser-Shmasser'. In February 1955, Israeli troops attacked and destroyed the Egyptian army headquarters in Gaza and killed 35 Egyptian soldiers. For the next three days Palestinian refugees in Gaza ran riot and demanded: 'Arms, give us arms, we shall defend ourselves!' In Cairo, the Egyptian capital, the crowds wanted revenge too.

The Israeli attack on Gaza was, as intended, humiliating for Nasser. He knew that it could have a very damaging effect on his leadership of Egypt and his image in the wider Arab world. He urgently needed arms to strengthen Egypt's army and deter any further Israeli attacks. His forces now began to arm and train *fedayeen* **guerrillas** to carry out attacks in Israel. What was most crucial, however, was that he secured Soviet arms. This he did through Soviet Russia's communist ally, Czechoslovakia. The Czech arms deal was announced in September 1955.

The importance of the Aswan Dam

This was a shock to the West, as well as to Israel. However, Britain and the USA thought they could still control Nasser because he depended on them for money to build the Aswan High Dam. This was a huge project on the River Nile which would create hydroelectric power for Egyptian industry and allow vast areas of agricultural land to be irrigated. It was proclaimed as a symbol of the new, dynamic Egypt which would allow the country to catch up with the West.

Meanwhile Nasser continued to show that he would not be pushed around and that Egypt was determined to be neutral. In May 1956, he recognised communist China. At this time, Western countries did not allow China to take its place at the UN and claimed that Taiwan, which was non-communist, represented China. In July 1956, the USA and Britain decided to cancel their loans to Egypt for the building of the Aswan Dam. Perhaps they hoped to persuade Nasser to be more co-operative. Maybe they thought they could force the Egyptians to replace him.

Key question
Why did the Israelis attack Gaza?

Key dates

Israeli attack on Gaza: February 1955

Egypt announced Czech arms deal: September 1955

Key term

Guerrillas
Soldiers who avoid fighting in open battle when possible; they prefer to use tactics like ambushes and hit-and-run raids.

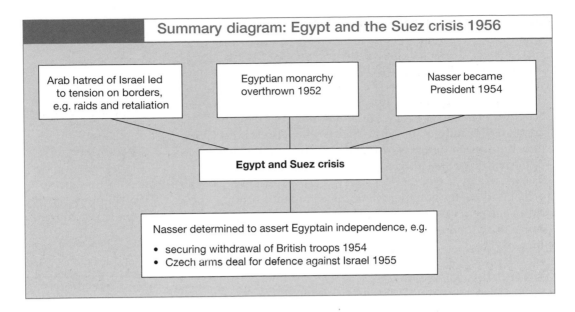

Summary diagram: Egypt and the Suez crisis 1956

Arab hatred of Israel led to tension on borders, e.g. raids and retaliation

Egyptian monarchy overthrown 1952

Nasser became President 1954

Egypt and Suez crisis

Nasser determined to assert Egyptain independence, e.g.

- securing withdrawal of British troops 1954
- Czech arms deal for defence against Israel 1955

2 | The Suez War 1956

Key question
Why did Britain, France and Israel decide to attack Egypt?

Yet again, however, Nasser shocked the West. He decided on a bold and defiant move to prove that Egypt really was independent. In front of a huge crowd, on 26 July, 1956, he announced that the Suez Canal was 'our Canal'. He told the crowd: 'We dug the Canal with our lives, our skulls, our bones, our blood.'

Key date
Nationalisation of Suez Canal: July 1956

> People of Egypt. We shall maintain our independence and sovereignty. The Suez Canal Company has become our property and the Egyptian flag flies over it. We shall defend it with our blood and strength, and we shall meet aggression with aggression and evil with evil.

Key terms

Nationalise
To transfer from private to government ownership.

Appease
To make concessions in order to avoid conflict.

Nasser decided that Egypt would **nationalise** the Canal and Egyptians would run it themselves. They would use the profits to build the Aswan Dam. He said that Britain and France could 'choke on their rage'. This daring act thrilled the Arabs in Egypt and elsewhere.

Britain and France were furious. The British Prime Minister, Anthony Eden, was determined not to let Nasser 'have his thumb on our windpipe'. The British and French withdrew their pilots who guided ships through the Canal. But the Egyptians kept it running and the traffic increased. The French saw Nasser as 'Hitler on the Nile'. They were determined not to **appease** Nasser as they had appeased Hitler in the 1930s. They had already agreed to sell Israel over 70 fighter planes and 200 tanks. Now they held secret meetings with the Israelis in order to plot Nasser's downfall. The French had an added reason for wishing to topple Nasser: they accused him of sending weapons and other aid to support the Algerians in their fight for independence from France.

In October the British joined the French and Israelis. On 24 October, the British and French Foreign Ministers secretly met the Israeli Prime Minister, David Ben-Gurion, in France. Ben-Gurion wished to end the border raids from Gaza and force Egypt to recognise the state of Israel. He also wanted to break the Egyptian **blockade** of the Tiran Straits which prevented Israeli ships from reaching the port of Eilat (see the map below). Furthermore, he was worried about the increasing military strength of Egypt and the fact that the armies of Egypt, Syria and Jordan had been put under the same command. Britain, France and Israel held further high-level meetings. Although it was denied at the time, a joint campaign against Egypt was being planned.

The fighting over Suez

On 29 October 1956, Israeli forces invaded Egypt. They advanced across Sinai towards the Suez Canal (see the map below). The next day, the governments of Britain and France ordered Egypt and Israel to cease fighting and withdraw 10 miles from the Canal. If either side refused, the British and French

Key question
What happened in the Suez War?

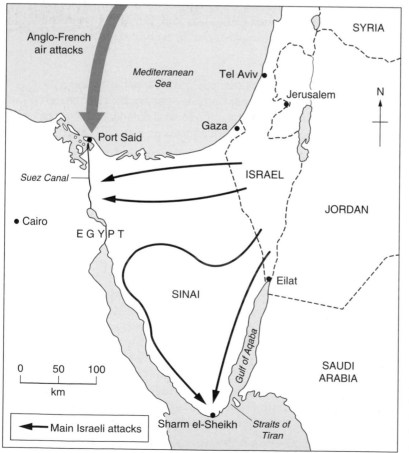

The 1956 Suez War. The Straits of Tiran were Israel's outlet to trade with Asia and Africa.

A British tank in Port Said.

 Key dates

Israeli forces invaded Egypt: 29 October 1956

British and French bombed Egyptian airfields: 31 October 1956

UN ceasefire and Anglo-French withdrawal from Egypt: 6 November 1956

would use force. The Israelis were still a long way from the Canal and they agreed but the Egyptians refused to withdraw from the Canal because it was Egyptian territory.

On 31 October, British and French planes bombed Egyptian airfields and destroyed most of their air force. They also bombed Port Said, the city at the northern end of the Canal (see the photograph above). On 5 November, British and French troops landed at Port Said and advanced along the Canal. Egypt responded by sinking ships, which had been filled with concrete, in order to obstruct the British and French advance along the Canal.

At the UN, the Arab states condemned the Anglo-French action. They halted oil supplies to the West. Even worse for Britain was the fact that its strongest ally, the USA, condemned the action. The US government was furious that Britain and France had used force. The Americans believed the Anglo-French action would lose the support of Arab states at a time when the USA was keen to win and make friends in the Arab world. The US government threatened to cut off financial aid to Britain, which would ruin the economy. The Soviet Union went further and threatened to use military force. On 6 November, the UN declared a ceasefire and ordered the British and French to withdraw. A UN emergency force was sent to the Canal.

Winners and losers in the Suez War

Nasser: hero of the Arab world

Key question
Who won and who lost the Suez War?

Nasser, the Egyptian leader, became the hero of the Arab world. He had stood up to Britain and France, who had dominated the Middle East for so long. He had gained complete control of the Suez Canal and of a large quantity of British military stores. With US aid the Canal was cleared and reopened in April 1957. Although Egypt lost territory when the Israelis captured Sinai, the Israelis were persuaded, by the Americans, to withdraw early in 1957. Besides, Nasser could claim that the Egyptian army had only been defeated because the Israelis had British and French support.

The Israelis

The Israelis also made gains. The speed of their victory over Egyptian forces in Gaza and Sinai had proved that the Israeli Defence Forces were the strongest in the Middle East. When they withdrew from Sinai, UN troops moved in to guard the border between Egypt and Israel. In particular, UN forces were sent to Gaza to prevent more raids on Israel and to Sharm-el-Sheikh (see map on page 42) to guard the passage of Israeli shipping through the Straits of Tiran.

Britain and France

The undoubted losers of the Suez War were Britain and France. They had failed to regain control of the Canal and they had failed to overthrow Nasser. The British lion was forced to slope off with its tail between its legs. The long period of Anglo-French domination of the Arab world was ending.

The effects of the war

One of the main effects of the Suez crisis was to make many of the Arab states more anti-Western than ever. Not only had Britain and France tried to overthrow the government of the leading Arab nation, but they had used Israel to do so. Now, more then ever before, Israel looked like an outpost of Western imperialism. The Arabs became more willing to seek Soviet aid. The Soviet Union now began to supply most of Egypt's weapons and to pay for the building of the Aswan Dam and many other projects. However, Nasser did not want Egypt to be tied to the Soviet Union and he was certainly not a communist. He wanted Egypt and the other Arab states to be neutral. (This is discussed more fully in Chapter 4.)

In 1964, Nasser invited the leaders of the Arab states to a conference in Cairo. Although many of them mistrusted each other, one thing united them all: opposition to the state of Israel and support for the Palestinians.

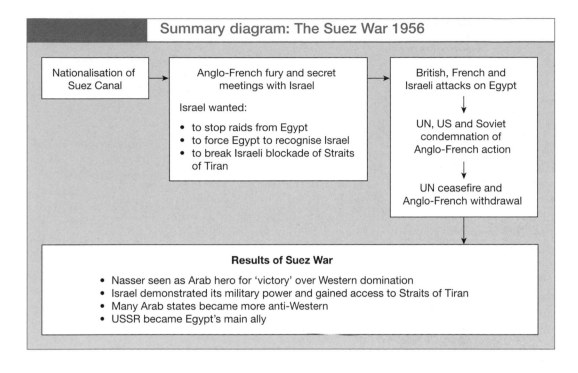

Summary diagram: The Suez War 1956

Nationalisation of Suez Canal

Anglo-French fury and secret meetings with Israel

Israel wanted:

- to stop raids from Egypt
- to force Egypt to recognise Israel
- to break Israeli blockade of Straits of Tiran

British, French and Israeli attacks on Egypt

↓

UN, US and Soviet condemnation of Anglo-French action

↓

UN ceasefire and Anglo-French withdrawal

Results of Suez War

- Nasser seen as Arab hero for 'victory' over Western domination
- Israel demonstrated its military power and gained access to Straits of Tiran
- Many Arab states became more anti-Western
- USSR became Egypt's main ally

3 | The Causes of the Six-Day War 1967

In its results the Six-Day War was the most dramatic of all the Arab–Israeli wars, yet it was the one that both sides wanted least. Before we study the events leading to war, we will look briefly at how Israel had developed since its creation as a new state.

The development of Israel

Key question
How did Israel develop into a strong, modern state?

Since the end of the war in 1949, the Israelis had lived with the threat of invasion. They knew they were surrounded by enemies and were convinced that the Arabs would try to attack again. Soon after the fighting had ended in 1949, the Secretary of the Arab League, which represents all Arab states, said:

> As long as we don't make peace with the Zionists the war is not over. And as long as the war is not over there is neither winner nor loser. As soon as we recognise the existence of Israel, we admit, by this act, that we are defeated.

Not surprisingly, the Israeli Defence Forces would have to be constantly on the alert. The Israeli army not only defended the new nation; it also helped to shape it. The Jews of Israel had come from different parts of Europe and the USA and, after 1949, nearly 700,000 new immigrants arrived. The 'Law of Return' gives any Jew in the world the right to become a citizen of Israel. Many of the new immigrants were from north Africa and other parts of the Middle East. In the army they all received a similar training, lived together and had to learn Hebrew, the

Jewish language. Experience in the army helped to make the newly arrived Jews into true Israelis.

Many Israelis went to live and work on **kibbutzim**. These were large co-operative farms in which all the property and work was shared. Different families ate together and shared living quarters. With financial aid from the USA and **reparations** from Germany, the Israelis irrigated and cultivated vast areas of desert.

The state of Israel became richer, stronger and more highly developed in the 1950s and early 1960s. New industries, such as cars, chemicals and defence, were built and vast sums of money were spent on the armed forces to defend the country. The high level of education and skills of Israeli citizens played a major part in this development but the speed of the country's progress would not have been possible without huge gifts from abroad. Most of this aid came from the USA. In fact, the US government and American Jews sent about a billion dollars a year to Israel. The US government felt that Israel was a close, firm friend in a troubled part of the world and it knew that the Soviet Union was arming Egypt and Syria. It also knew that the Arab states were united in their opposition to the state of Israel.

Key terms

Kibbutzim
Settlements in Israel where people live and work together.

Reparations
Damages or compensation which Germany paid to Israel for the persecution of the Jews during the Second World War.

The Palestine Liberation Organisation (PLO)

At their meeting in Cairo in 1964, the leaders of the Arab states had stated:

Key question
What part did Fatah play in the developing conflict between Israel and its Arab neighbours?

> The existence of Israel is a danger that threatens the Arab nation. Collective Arab military preparations, when they are completed, will constitute the ultimate practical means for the final liquidation of Israel.

This may have been just rhetoric, or bold talk, to enable the Arab states to show a united front but it was the first time that they had declared, in an official document, that their ultimate aim was the destruction of Israel. The Arab leaders went on to set up the Palestine Liberation Organisation (PLO) whose aim was to win back the land which the Palestinians had lost in 1948–9. In 1965 a guerrilla group called **Fatah**, which was part of the PLO, carried out its first raid on Israel. Fatah had its bases in three of the Arab countries that bordered Israel: Syria, Jordan and Lebanon. This group carried out many armed raids into Israel over the next few years. Israeli retaliation for Fatah raids was usually swift and harsh.

The governments of Lebanon and Jordan tried to restrict PLO activities because they were afraid of Israeli reprisals. The Syrians, however, were keen to support the PLO. They encouraged Fatah's raids against Israel and supplied men and arms. The only neighbouring state from which Israel was not attacked was Egypt. This was because UN troops had been placed on the border between Egypt and Israel after the 1956 war to prevent further clashes.

Key term

Fatah
A Palestinian guerrilla group founded by Yasser Arafat. Its general strategy was to drag the Arab states into war with Israel so that a Palestinian state might be established.

Key dates

Palestine Liberation Organisation (PLO) established: 1964

Fatah carried out its first raid on Israel: 1965

Key dates

Egypt signed a defence agreement with Syria: 1966

Air fight between Israeli and Syrian planes: 7 April 1967

Countdown to war, April 1966–7

In February 1966 a new, radical and aggressive government came to power in Syria. It demanded 'revolutionary struggle' against Israel and called for the 'liberation of Palestine'. The Syrians now stepped up their support for the PLO guerrillas and accused the Egyptian government of not supporting them. Nasser was stung, but he did not want war: he knew that the Arab states were not ready and that Israel had stronger military forces than all the neighbouring Arab states combined. Besides, many of his best troops were at war in Yemen (see page 71). Yet he wanted to remain the leader of the Arab world, the champion of Arab nationalism. So, in November 1966, he signed a defence agreement with the Syrian government whereby, if one state was attacked, the other would come to its defence. Nasser hoped the pact would restrain the hotheads in the Syrian government but all it did was encourage them.

Tension was high not only in Syria for a week after the Egyptian–Syrian pact was signed, a mine exploded on the Israel–Jordan frontier, killing three Israeli soldiers. The Israelis retaliated with a massive attack on the Jordanian village of Samu from which they believed the attackers had come. Fifteen Jordanian troops and three civilians were killed and over 100 houses destroyed. In early 1967 there were many more raids and reprisals across the borders. Tension was particularly high on the Israeli–Syrian border: several of Israel's military leaders were keen to provoke clashes with Syria so that they could retaliate forcefully and teach the Syrians a lesson. One particular incident illustrates this.

On 7 April 1967 an Israeli tractor was ploughing land in the demilitarised zone. The Syrians opened fire and the Israelis fired back. The Syrians then started shelling other Israeli settlements in the area. Israeli tanks went into action but could not reach all the positions from which the Syrians had been firing. So Israeli planes were called up. These were then intercepted by Syrian fighter planes and, in the air fight which ensued, six Syrian planes were shot down, two of them over the Syrian capital. The Israeli planes roared low over Damascus, further humiliating the Syrians. Some historians believe that this incident started the countdown to the Six-Day War in June 1967. Many years later, the Israeli leader, Moshe Dayan, explained in an interview that Israel provoked 'at least 80 per cent' of the clashes on the border.

Key question
Who was to blame for the outbreak of war in June 1967?

The crisis of May 1967

By May 1967 Israel and its Arab enemies were sliding into a crisis that neither side could control. Israel issued several threats to act against Syria unless it stopped supporting Palestinian attacks on Israel. On 12 May an Israeli general threatened to occupy the Syrian capital, Damascus, and overthrow the Syrian government. He was severely criticised by the Israeli government but his words were widely interpreted by the Arabs as a sign that Israel intended to attack Syria.

Then the USSR intervened. The Soviet government regarded Syria as a key ally in the Middle East. On 13 May the Soviets warned the Egyptian government that Israel was moving its armed forces to the border with Syria, Egypt's ally, and was planning to attack. This was not true. Moreover, Nasser knew the Soviet report was untrue. The Soviets were either mistaken or were lying. Perhaps they saw an opportunity to expand their influence in the region at a time when the USA was bogged down in **Vietnam**.

Nevertheless, the story spread rapidly. Arab eyes were on Nasser. What would he do? He did not want war as he knew that Israeli forces were far superior to those of the Arab states yet he had to respond because his leadership of the Arab world was being challenged. Since the attack on Samu, the Jordanians had been accusing Nasser of cowardice and of hiding behind the protection of the UN troops. Besides, he had a defence agreement with Syria compelling Egypt to go to Syria's aid if Syria was attacked by Israel. As the historian Avi Shlaim put it: 'What he did was to embark on an exercise in **brinkmanship** that was to carry him over the brink.'

Key terms

Vietnam
The USA had a large military force fighting against communist North Vietnam and its communist allies in South Vietnam.

Brinkmanship
Pursuing a dangerous policy to the limits of safety.

Nasser's next moves
Nasser took three steps, both to deter Israel and to impress Arab public opinion:

- First, on 15 May he moved 100,000 Egyptian troops into Sinai (see the map on page 52). This was Egyptian territory but it alarmed the Israelis because it brought Egyptian troops nearer to Israel.
- Secondly, he asked the UN commander to remove his troops from Egyptian soil. He wanted to prove that Egypt was completely independent. The UN forces could stay on Egyptian territory only as long as Egypt allowed them. The UN Secretary-General proposed that the UN troops be placed on

Key date

Nasser moved Egyptian troops into Sinai: 15 May 1967

A cartoon published in a Lebanese Arab newspaper in May 1967. Each cannon has the name of a different Arab state on it, but Egypt is not one of them. What is the message of the cartoon? Why do you think the name of Egypt is omitted?

Nasser closed the
Straits of Tiran to
Israeli shipping:
22 May 1967

Jordan signed a
defence treaty with
Egypt: 30 May 1967

the Israeli side of the border but the Israelis refused, so the UN troops were withdrawn.
• Thirdly, on 22 May Nasser closed the Straits of Tiran, which led into the Gulf of Aqaba, to Israeli shipping (see the map on page 52). The Israelis regarded this as 'an act of aggression' against Israel, and claimed that the USA, France and Britain had 'guaranteed' free passage for all shipping through the Gulf of Aqaba in 1957.

Meanwhile, a war fever was being whipped up in the press and radio in several Arab states. On 24 May 1967 the Syrian Defence Minister challenged the Israelis: 'We shall never call for, nor accept peace. We have resolved to drench this land with your blood and throw you into the sea for good.'

Israel's response

Among the Israeli public, many feared a repeat of 1948 as the country was surrounded by warlike Arab states. Israeli military leaders knew that an Arab invasion was not imminent but were now keen to go to war and they were confident of victory. However, the Israeli government insisted on securing US support: they needed, for example, to be sure that the US government would stand by Israel in the UN if Israel attacked first. The US President told the Israelis that, according to US intelligence, Egypt had no plan to attack but that, if it did, then the Israelis would 'whip the hell out of them'. He then added: 'Israel will not be alone unless it decides to go it alone'. The Israeli government decided to wait.

Increased pressure on Israel

In Egypt, on 29 May, Nasser stepped up the pressure in a speech to the Egyptian parliament:

> We are now ready to confront Israel. The issue now at hand is not the Gulf of Aqaba, the Straits of Tiran, or the withdrawal of the UN forces, but the rights of the Palestine people. It is the aggression which took place in Palestine in 1948 with the collaboration of Britain and the United States.

He demanded that Israel should allow the Palestinian refugees to return to Israel and that Israel should give up the land taken in the 1948–9 war. Perhaps he thought that Israel would give way and he could win a victory without a war. In Jordan, King Hussein wanted to avoid war and remain neutral if fighting broke out. But half the population of Jordan was Palestinian, and newspapers and demonstrations demanded revenge for what had happened in 1948–9. On 30 May King Hussein signed a defence treaty with Egypt.

On 31 May, a second Israeli delegation went to Washington. They wanted the US government to take action to open the Straits of Tiran. The Americans suggested that Israel should take action, on its own, to open the Straits. This was taken as a sign to go ahead and take military action.

Just after dawn on Monday 5 June, the Israeli air force took off. It attacked the Arab planes on the ground: within four hours the Israelis had destroyed the air forces of Egypt, Syria and Jordan. The war was to last six days but the Israelis had virtually won on the first day. They had complete control of the skies.

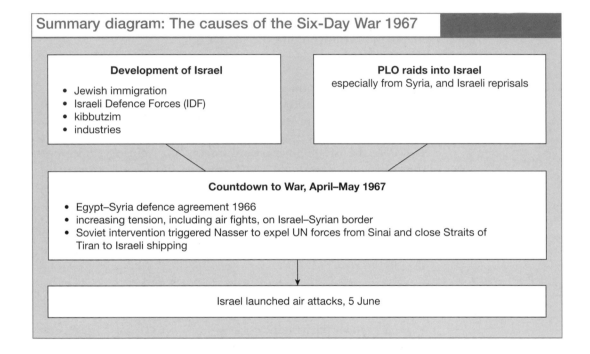

Summary diagram: The causes of the Six-Day War 1967

Development of Israel
- Jewish immigration
- Israeli Defence Forces (IDF)
- kibbutzim
- industries

PLO raids into Israel
especially from Syria, and Israeli reprisals

Countdown to War, April–May 1967
- Egypt–Syria defence agreement 1966
- increasing tension, including air fights, on Israel–Syrian border
- Soviet intervention triggered Nasser to expel UN forces from Sinai and close Straits of Tiran to Israeli shipping

Israel launched air attacks, 5 June

4 | The Six-Day War and its Results

The fighting on three fronts, June 1967
The main facts of the fighting are presented in Table 3.1 on page 51.

The results of the Six-Day War
Israeli triumph
The Israelis won a spectacular military victory and were now the dominant power in the Middle East. The Arabs had lost 15,000 men while the Israelis had lost fewer than a thousand. The Arabs had larger armies but their air forces were destroyed. The Arabs had modern Soviet missiles and other weapons but the Israelis had French fighter planes and tanks. The Israelis also had the most advanced US electronic equipment, which enabled them to intercept Arab communications, and they were highly skilled and well trained. Above all, the Israelis believed they were fighting for their nation's survival.

Key question
What were the results of the Six-Day War?

Six-Day War:
5–10 June 1967

Key date

Table 3.1 A summary of the Six-Day War

Date	Israel vs Egypt	Israel vs Jordan	Israel vs Syria
Monday 5 June	Israeli planes bombed all 19 Egyptian airfields and wrecked 300 planes. Israeli troops advanced into the Gaza Strip and Sinai desert.	The Israelis destroyed the Jordanian air force. Jordanian troops attacked west Jerusalem.	Israeli planes crippled the Syrian air force.
Tuesday 6 June	The Israelis raced the Egyptian forces to the Suez Canal. The Israeli air force destroyed many tanks and other vehicles, while Israeli ground forces destroyed or captured the rest.	Heavy fighting for control of Jerusalem and the West Bank of the River Jordan.	
Wednesday 7 June	The Israelis won complete control of Sinai and accepted the UN call for a ceasefire with Egypt.	The Israelis captured all of Jerusalem. Jordan accepted the UN demand for a ceasefire.	
Thursday 8 June	Egypt accepted the ceasefire call.	Israel won control of all the West Bank of the River Jordan.	
Friday 9 June			Israeli troops attacked the Golan Heights.
Saturday 10 June			Israelis took control of the Golan Heights. Syria accepted the UN call for a ceasefire.

After their success in the war, the Israelis had to decide what to do with the lands they had conquered. These were the West Bank, Gaza, Sinai and the Golan Heights. For the time being, the Israeli government decided on military occupation. These **occupied territories** were to become the central issue in Arab–Israeli relations for the next 40 years. Control of these lands made Israel's borders more secure. There was a buffer zone between its land and each of its three main enemies (as you can see on the map on page 52):

- Villages in the north of Israel were safe from Syrian artillery now that the Israelis controlled the Golan Heights.
- Military fortifications were built on the banks of the River Jordan while the land on the West Bank of the river was controlled by Israel.
- The Sinai desert formed a huge buffer between Israel and the Egyptian army.

The Israeli government later ordered the army to confiscate Arab land and to build Jewish **settlements** in order to make the areas more secure.

Key terms

Occupied territories
Lands controlled by the troops of a foreign power (in this case, the West Bank, Gaza, Sinai and Golan Heights, all occupied by Israeli troops).

Settlement
A group of houses, as built by the Israelis on the West Bank and in Gaza.

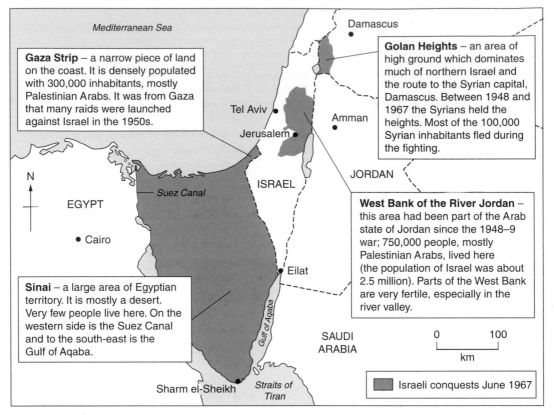

The occupied territories.

On one point, in particular, the Israelis were united. They had taken control of east Jerusalem, the Old City, for the first time in nearly 2000 years. They were determined to hold on to it. As the Israeli Defence Minister, General Dayan, said on the radio: 'We have unified Jerusalem, the divided capital of Israel. We have returned to the holiest of our holy places, never to part from it again.'

The Arabs in defeat

The Arabs felt more hostile than ever. They blamed their defeat on the USA, Britain and other European powers, whom they accused of helping Israel in the war. The three main oil-producing Arab states of Saudi Arabia, Kuwait and Libya agreed to pay £135 million annually to Egypt and Jordan as compensation for their suffering in the war. The Soviet Union decided to replace the weapons which its allies, Egypt and Syria, had lost. Meanwhile the Arab leaders, at a conference in August 1967, declared: 'No peace with Israel, no recognition of Israel, no negotiation with it. We insist on the rights of the Palestinian people in their country.'

UN Resolution 242:
November 1967

UN Resolution 242

In November 1967, the UN passed Resolution 242 which called for permanent peace based on:

- 'The withdrawal of Israeli armed forces from the territories occupied in the recent conflict.'
- Respect for the right of every state in the area 'to live in peace within secure and recognised boundaries, free from threats or acts of force'.

The Resolution supported the Arabs on the issue of land and supported Israel on the issue of peace and security. Egypt and Jordan accepted the Resolution, effectively recognising Israel's right to exist. Israel held up the 'three noes' of the Arab conference in August as proof that the Arabs did not really want a peace settlement, but the Israeli government eventually accepted the resolution. The UN led discussions with the warring parties but made little progress: Israel found that its occupation of Arab land gave it added security while the Arabs insisted on Israeli withdrawal as a first step to peace.

Many subsequent peace discussions were to be based on the formula of land for peace, most notably those leading to a peace treaty between Israel and Egypt in 1979 (see page 58). But before that, there was to be another war between Israel and its Arab neighbours.

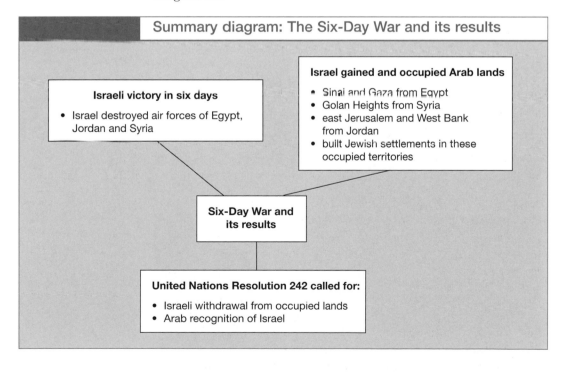

Summary diagram: The Six-Day War and its results

Israeli victory in six days

- Israel destroyed air forces of Egypt, Jordan and Syria

Israel gained and occupied Arab lands

- Sinai and Gaza from Egypt
- Golan Heights from Syria
- east Jerusalem and West Bank from Jordan
- built Jewish settlements in these occupied territories

Six-Day War and its results

United Nations Resolution 242 called for:

- Israeli withdrawal from occupied lands
- Arab recognition of Israel

5 | From War to Peace: Yom Kippur to Camp David 1973–8

At the end of the Six-Day War in 1967 there was no peace treaty. In fact, fighting broke out again in 1968 between Israel and Egypt over the Suez Canal. The Egyptians wished to clear the Canal of sunken ships but the Israelis, who now occupied Sinai, would only agree to this if Egypt allowed their ships through the Canal. Over the next two years there were many clashes across the Canal. Both Egypt and Israel lost many men and weapons and, by 1970, both sides were tiring. Nasser had not received the support he had hoped for from other Arab states nor had he managed to dislodge the Israelis. Meanwhile, Egyptian cities on the Canal were regularly pulverised by Israeli guns in this '**war of attrition**'.

President Sadat and the origins of the war

In September 1970 Nasser died and was succeeded by his Vice-President, Anwar Sadat. Like Nasser, Sadat had been an army officer. He realised that the fighting over the Suez Canal was draining Egypt of money and morale. The Canal could not be used and fighting could flare up at any time. Egypt had to keep nearly a million men ready to fight and this was very expensive. Peace was needed in order to clear the Canal and rebuild Egypt's cities. However, the overriding objective for Egypt was to regain Sinai, the land which it had lost in 1967. Sadat promised his people that the year 1971 'would not end without the conflict with Israel having been settled'.

'No peace, no war'

Sadat was prepared to recognise the state of Israel in order to regain the lost land. However, the Israelis were unwilling to discuss it and Sadat knew he could not defeat Israel in war. He also knew that only the USA could force Israel to enter into peace

Key question
Why did Egypt and Syria attack Israel in 1973?

Key term

War of attrition
A war in which each side tries to wear the other out.

Key date

Anwar Sadat became President of Egypt: 1970

President Sadat of Egypt. He promised to settle the conflict with Israel.

discussions: as he said, the Americans hold 99 per cent of the cards in the Middle East. Sadat realised that the US government wanted peace and friendship with the Arab states in the Middle East. As an Arab, he hoped he could persuade the US government to use its influence with the Israelis. He sacked the members of his government who were anti-American. The USA, however, was too busy with the war in Vietnam. Besides, the six million Jews in America would oppose any attempt by the US government to 'bully' the Israelis. So the year 1971 ended, as it had begun, with 'no peace, no war'.

Sadat continued to secure aircraft and arms from the Soviet Union but they would not provide Egypt with the type of equipment it needed to make a successful attack across the Canal possible. More significantly, the Soviets could not exert any leverage over the Israelis. In 1972, Sadat expelled all 15,000 Soviet advisers who had been training Egypt's armed forces. This was a popular move as Soviet interference in Egyptian affairs had been resented, especially by the army. This still made little difference to the United States' attitude.

In 1972, Sadat decided that the stalemate could only be broken by war. He knew that weaponry, training and planning in the army had been much improved, especially with Soviet aid, but he would need further support from abroad in order to force the Israelis out of Sinai. He now had strong financial support from the oil-rich state of Saudi Arabia. Also, the new Syrian leader, President Assad, became a close ally. Both Sadat and Assad realised that they would have to act soon if they were to recover Sinai and the Golan Heights, the lands they had lost in 1967. The Israelis were increasing their control of these areas: they were building new Jewish settlements and kept many troops there. Secretly, the Egyptian and Syrian leaders prepared for war. In September, Sadat made a defiant speech in Cairo:

The United States is still under Zionist pressure and is wearing Zionist spectacles. The United States will have to take off those spectacles before they talk to us. We have had enough talk. We know our goal and we are determined to attain it.

Very few people took his speech seriously. They had heard it all before. So had the Israelis, who had a low opinion of the Arab armies anyway. They were in for a shock.

The fighting, October 1973

On 6 October Egypt and Syria attacked. It was **Yom Kippur**, a holiday and the holiest day of the Jewish year. This meant that many soldiers were on leave. The Israelis were caught completely by surprise. Over 90,000 Egyptian soldiers and 850 tanks crossed the Suez Canal in the first 24 hours, destroying 300 Israeli tanks and regaining part of Sinai. The whole operation had been planned and practised very thoroughly. At the same time, 500 Syrian tanks overwhelmed Israeli forces on the Golan Heights. The Israeli air force retaliated but discovered that the Arabs had

Key term

Yom Kippur
Day of Atonement, an important Jewish religious day of fasting and an annual Jewish holiday.

Key question
What happened in the early stages of the war?

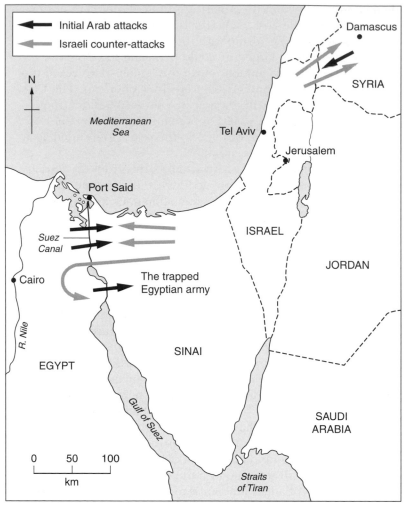

The Yom Kippur War, 1973.

Soviet surface-to-air missiles which they used very effectively. It took the Israeli army three days to become fully mobilised. However, by 12 October, they had pushed the Syrians back and, on 15 October, they thrust across the Suez Canal and cut off the Egyptian third army (see the above map).

Yom Kippur War: 6–24 October 1973 | Key date

The oil weapon

With the Israelis threatening the Egyptian capital, Cairo, the Arabs produced an unexpected weapon – oil. The West received much of its oil from the Middle East. The Arab oil-producing states decided to reduce oil production until the Israelis withdrew from the lands they had occupied in 1967. The richest oil state, Saudi Arabia, went further. It banned all oil exports to the USA and to the Netherlands, which supplied much of Western Europe through the port of Rotterdam. The West was shocked.

Key question
Why and how did the superpowers become involved?

The superpowers intervene

The USA and the USSR were deeply involved in the Yom Kippur War. The USSR sent arms to Egypt and Syria and the USA organised a massive airlift to Israel. When the Israelis crossed the Suez Canal both superpowers stepped in. The Soviet government advised Egypt to accept a ceasefire while it still held part of Sinai. The US government, for its part, was worried by the Arab oil weapon, but even more by the threat of armed intervention by Soviet troops. For a time, American forces were put on nuclear alert.

Both superpowers were keen to avoid a direct confrontation. The USA prevented its Israeli ally from advancing on either Cairo or Damascus, the Syrian capital. American and Soviet leaders met and together demanded a ceasefire which the UN supported. The fighting ended on 24 October. A few days later UN troops were sent to Egypt to preserve the ceasefire.

Key question
To what extent was the war an Arab victory?

The results of the war

The Yom Kippur War was, in the end, a military victory for the Israelis. Yet again they had proved that their weapons, their training and their tactics were superior. But they had incurred far more losses, of both men and weaponry, than in previous wars. Perhaps most significant, the Arabs had destroyed the myth of Israeli invincibility. They had completely surprised the Israelis and the rest of the world with their attack. They had proved that Arab soldiers could fight with courage and determination under skilled leaders. Above all, they had acted together, both in their military planning and in the use of the oil weapon. As a result the rest of the world showed much more respect for the Arabs.

One man, in particular, emerged from the war as a world leader. Anwar Sadat had achieved exactly what he had set out to do. First, he had broken the stalemate that existed before the war. Secondly, he had forced a change in US policy. From now on, the USA was to become far more friendly towards the Arab states and far more willing to persuade Israel to enter peace negotiations.

Key question
What steps led to an Israeli–Egyptian peace treaty?

President Sadat and the Israeli–Egyptian peace treaty

For the next two years, from 1973 to 1975, the US Secretary of State, Henry Kissinger, engaged in 'shuttle diplomacy': he shuttled back and forth between the Israeli, Egyptian and Syrian capitals in order to arrange treaties of 'disengagement'. In 1974–5 he secured a series of agreements by which Israeli forces would withdraw from the Suez Canal area and from part of the Golan Heights. The agreement on Suez enabled Egypt to clear the Canal, which was reopened in 1975, and to start rebuilding the cities along the Canal which had been devastated by Israeli shelling from 1968 to 1970. Saudi Arabia started selling oil to the USA again.

Sadat flies to Israel 1977

The bravest peacemaker, however, was undoubtedly President Sadat. He wanted permanent peace because four wars against Israel had cost many lives and devastated the Egyptian economy. Egypt needed a lasting peace in order to recover. In November 1977 he surprised the world by announcing that he was willing to go to Israel and discuss peace. This was a bold move because, for 30 years, no Arab leader had even agreed to recognise Israel's existence. Ten days later he flew to Israel. He spoke to the Israeli parliament:

> We used to reject you, and we had our reasons and grievances. But I say to you today and I say to the whole world that we accept that we should live with you in lasting and just peace.

In his reply, the Israeli Prime Minister said:

> The time of the flight from Cairo to Jerusalem is short but the distance until last night was almost infinite.

The following month the Israeli Prime Minister, Menachem Begin, went to Egypt and peace talks were started. When they slowed down in 1978, US President Carter invited the Egyptian and Israeli leaders to **Camp David** in the USA. For 13 days the three men and their advisers discussed a peace settlement.

Camp David
The US President's mountain retreat.

Key term

Agreement at Camp David 1978

At Camp David, a framework for peace between Israel and Egypt was agreed. The main points were:

Key question
What were the results of the Camp David meeting?

- Israeli forces to be withdrawn from Sinai
- Egypt to regain all of Sinai within three years
- Israeli shipping to have free passage through the Suez Canal and the Straits of Tiran (see the map on page 56).

Camp David Agreement between Egypt and Israel: 1978

Treaty of Washington between Egypt and Israel: 1979

Key dates

The Treaty of Washington 1979

Six months after Camp David, in March 1979, the Egyptian and Israeli leaders signed the Treaty of Washington which confirmed what they had agreed at Camp David. Both sides finally agreed to recognise 'each other's right to live in peace within their secure and recognised boundaries'.

The Israelis felt more secure now that they had traded land for peace and neutralised the biggest Arab military power. Most Egyptians were pleased that Sadat was putting Egypt's interests first: they felt that Egypt had made huge sacrifices in blood and money on behalf of the Arabs. In fact, most of the world applauded this breakthrough in Arab–Israeli relations. But that was not how the rest of the Arab world viewed things: they saw Sadat as breaking Arab ranks. Instead of standing up to Israel

Key date

Assassination of
President Sadat:
1981

and the West, as Nasser had done, he had sold out. The Arab states cut off all relations with Egypt and moved the headquarters of the Arab League from Cairo to Tunisia.

Furthermore, even among the Egyptians, there was a small minority, mainly Islamic activists, who turned against Sadat for making peace with the Zionist enemy and for his hostility to the Islamic Revolution in Iran (see Chapter 7). In 1981, during a military parade in Cairo, Sadat was assassinated by a group of Islamic extremists within the army.

It was to be 15 years before another Arab state made peace with Israel. Meanwhile, at the heart of the conflict in the Middle East, there still remained the Palestinian problem. This is the subject of the next chapter.

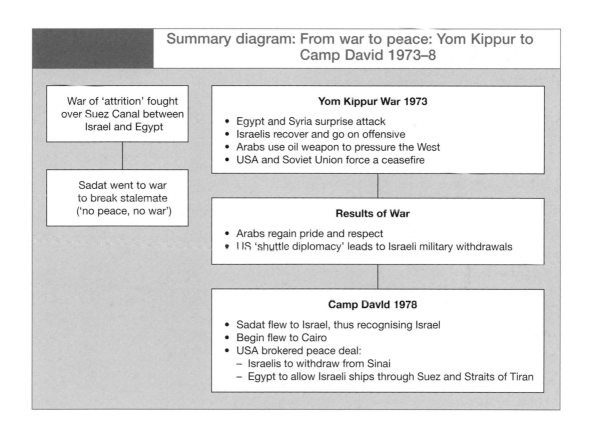

Summary diagram: From war to peace: Yom Kippur to Camp David 1973–8

War of 'attrition' fought over Suez Canal between Israel and Egypt

Sadat went to war to break stalemate ('no peace, no war')

Yom Kippur War 1973
- Egypt and Syria surprise attack
- Israelis recover and go on offensive
- Arabs use oil weapon to pressure the West
- USA and Soviet Union force a ceasefire

Results of War
- Arabs regain pride and respect
- US 'shuttle diplomacy' leads to Israeli military withdrawals

Camp David 1978
- Sadat flew to Israel, thus recognising Israel
- Begin flew to Cairo
- USA brokered peace deal:
  - Israelis to withdraw from Sinai
  - Egypt to allow Israeli ships through Suez and Straits of Tiran

Study Guide

In the style of Edexcel and OCR

How far do you agree that the *main* cause of the Arab–Israeli wars of 1948–9, 1967 and 1973 was the Arab desire to destroy the state of Israel?

Exam tips

The cross-references are intended to take you straight to the material that will help you to answer the question.

In this essay you need to assess the importance of the Arab desire to destroy the state of Israel in relation to other factors before making a judgement about whether it was the main factor. It is probably best to analyse each war in turn, identifying the main factors leading to war and then pull together your overarching assessment.

The 1948–9 war (pages 20–9)
The invasion by Arab armies suggests that the desire to destroy the new state was the main cause but were there other factors, even if less important? You might consider:

- retaliation for the expulsion of Palestinian Arabs from lands allocated to Israel
- the evidence which suggests that Transjordan, with the strongest Arab military force, did not wish to destroy Israel.

The 1967 war (pages 45–50)
Israel actually launched the attack in June but was it acting defensively? You need to analyse:

- The policies and actions of the main players, i.e. Syria, Jordan and Egypt. Evidence suggests that Syria was more intent on destroying Israel than the other two states.
- The importance of the PLO and Arab support for their guerrilla raids on Israel.
- The role of the radio, press and popular opinion in the Arab countries.
- Might Israel have launched the war in order to deter the Arab states from supporting Fatah attacks inside Israel? Or, to teach Syria a lesson or to force the Arab states to acknowledge Israel's permanence?

Making firm conclusions may be difficult. You have to make the best judgements you can based on the evidence.

The 1973 war (pages 54–7)
You need to ask yourself:
- Did Syria and Egypt attack in order to destroy Israel?
- Or did they attack to regain lands they had lost in 1967?

- Did Sadat think war alone would enable Egypt to regain lost land or did Egypt go to war to force a change in US policy in the Middle East?
- Were Egypt and Syria, supported by oil-rich Arab states, motivated by a desire to regain their honour, and show new-found strength and unity, after the humiliating defeat of 1967?

In your conclusion, you should identify:

- the wars in which you think the Arab desire to destroy Israel was the main factor
- wars in which other causes were more important.

You will then need to reach an overall judgement. Stronger answers will look to identify differences in motivation between different Arab states.

In the style of the International Baccalaureate

Source A

Extract from: The Arab–Israeli Wars, *1982, by C. Herzog.*

Syrian attacks along the northern frontier continued, as did infiltration into Israel from Syrian-based camps, via Jordan and Lebanon. In April 1967, their shelling of farming operations in the demilitarised zones along the Sea of Galilee [in northern Israel] were stepped up, with increasing fire being directed against Israeli border villages. On 7 April 1967, unusually heavy fire was directed by long-range guns against Israeli villages, and Israeli aircraft were sent into action against them.

Source B

Speaking in an interview in 1976, the Israeli leader, Moshe Dayan, explained how tension on the Israeli–Syrian border had escalated in the weeks leading up to outbreak of the Six-Day War.

I know how at least 80 per cent of the clashes there started. It went this way: we would send a tractor to plough some place where it wasn't possible to do anything, in the demilitarised area, and knew in advance that the Syrians would start to shoot. If they didn't shoot, we would tell the tractor to advance further, until in the end the Syrians would get annoyed and shoot. And then we would use artillery and later the air force also, and that's how it was.

Source C

Ahmed Said speaking on 'Voice of the Arabs' radio in Cairo. This radio station was used to broadcast Nasser's speeches (quoted in Six Days, *by J. Bowen, 2003).*

We have nothing for Israel except war – comprehensive war … marching against its gangs, destroying and putting an end to the whole Zionist existence. Our aim is to destroy the myth which says that Israel is here to stay. Everyone of the 100 million Arabs has been living for the past 19 years on one hope – to live, to die on the day Israel is liquidated. There is no life, no peace or hope for the gangs of Zionism to remain in the occupied land.

Source D

A young Fatah member being trained in the use of his weapon.

Source E

From a booklet published by the Israeli government in 1969.

In 1966–7 terrorism had been increased by the Arab states to a fearsome peak. Syrian radio continuously broadcast claims of the havoc and destruction caused by Arab terrorists in Israel. The Syrian Prime Minister said at the United Nations in October 1966: 'Syria will never retreat from the popular liberation war to recover Palestine.'

(a) (i) What does the author of Source A mean by 'infiltration into Israel from Syrian-based camps'? (2 marks)

(ii) What is the significance of what the Syrian Prime Minister is quoted as saying in Source E? (3 marks)

(b) In what ways do Sources B and D support the views expressed in Source A? (6 marks)

(c) With reference to their origins and purpose, assess the value and limitations of Sources C and E for the historian studying the causes of the Six-Day War. (6 marks)

(d) Using these sources and your own knowledge, assess the causes of the Six-Day War. (8 marks)

Exam tips

Read pages 45–50 again.

(a) (i) This source is referring to attacks by Fatah from Palestinian refugee camps in Syria.

(ii) According to this Israeli government source, the Syrian leader is saying that Syria will continue to support the 'popular liberation war to recover Palestine', probably referring to the PLO campaign, led by Fatah guerrillas, to win back all of the land lost in 1948–9. That would mean the elimination of the state of Israel. He is making the claim in the very public international arena of the UN.

(b) Source A writes of increasing attacks by Syria and of Palestinian 'infiltration' of Israel. The author refers to the shelling of Israeli villages in the demilitarised zones. In Source B the Israeli leader writes of sending tractors into the demilitarised areas, similar to Source A's reference to 'farming operations' in those areas, but suggests that the Israelis deliberately provoked the Syrians into shooting by ploughing in areas 'where it wasn't possible to do anything' and telling 'the tractor to advance further' so that the Syrians 'would get annoyed and shoot'. By contrast, Source A makes no mention of any Israeli blame. Both refer to the use of Israeli aircraft but only Source A implies that it was for purely defensive purposes. Source D shows a Fatah member, one of the PLO fighters, receiving military training, presumably for attacks on Israel. This would seem to support Source A's reference to 'infiltration into Israel from Syrian-based camps', as we know Syria supported the PLO campaign to regain Palestine. However, there is no indication that Fatah fighters were involved in the shelling that Source A refers to.

(c) Source C comes from Cairo radio which was used to broadcast Nasser's speeches which suggests that it was government controlled and that these views were, at least, condoned by the government. This source expresses hatred of Israel and suggests that 'everyone of the 100 million Arabs' wishes to destroy the Zionist state. That may be an exaggeration, but may equally be representative of intense anti-Israeli feeling in Egypt, if not across the Arab world. Alternatively, it may indicate an Egyptian government desire to whip up anti-Israeli feeling, possibly in preparation for war, or just to be perceived to be reflecting popular opinion. So the source is probably of value in indicating official and popular opinion of Israel in Egypt at this time.

For Source E, you should comment on who published it and when. The date of publication might suggest what its purpose was. This in turn might suggest its value and limitations as evidence for the causes of the War. Do you think it is exaggerated? If so, which parts and why?

(d) It is best to group the sources into those that blame Israel and those that blame the Arabs.

- Source A blames Syria and, by implication, the Fatah fighters of the PLO, for attacks on Israel. It refers to increasing firing in April 1967.
- Source C suggests that war fever was being whipped up by Egyptian radio while Source D illustrates Fatah training for attacks on Israel.
- Source E reinforces Source A in blaming Syria and refers to use of the radio, this time in Syria, to intensify warlike, anti-Israeli feeling.
- Source B, surprisingly from an Israeli, suggests a deliberate Israeli policy of provoking the Syrians into armed conflict. It is taken from an interview nine years later but its reliability is suggested by the fact that it comes from an Israeli leader.

Using your own knowledge, you might refer to long-term causes like the defeat of Arab forces and expulsion of Palestinian Arabs in 1948–9 (hinted at in Source C's reference to 'the past 19 years') which gave many Arabs a motive for going to war. Memories of 1948–9 and the invasion of Israel by Arab forces also intensified Israeli fears for their country's survival which played a part in Israel's decision to go to war in June. You might also refer to the involvement of Soviet Russia and the USA in the events of May 1967.

4 Nasser, Egypt and Arab Nationalism

POINTS TO CONSIDER

This chapter traces the growth of Arab nationalism, which was closely linked with the name of Nasser, President of Egypt from 1954 until his death in 1970. It examines Nasser's defiance of the West, his undisputed leadership of the Arab world, the union of Egypt and Syria and the gradual decline of Arab nationalism. These are examined under the following headings:

- The growth of Arab nationalism
- The United Arab Republic 1958–61

Key dates

1945	Formation of Arab League
1955	Baghdad Pact formed
	Nasser announced Czech arms deal
1956	Suez crisis
1958	Formation of the United Arab Republic (UAR)
1961	Syria left the UAR
1962–7	Nasser sent military aid to the Yemen
1964	Conference of Arab leaders in Cairo
	Formation of the Palestine Liberation Organisation (PLO)
1967	Six-Day War
1970	Death of Nasser

1 | The Growth of Arab Nationalism

Key question
Why did Arab nationalism emerge as a political movement?

Arab nationalism
A movement striving for Arab political unity.

In the early twentieth century the Arabs sought independence from European colonial rule. Countries such as Syria, Lebanon and Palestine were ruled by the Turks while Egypt was dominated by the British. Many Arabs embraced the idea of **Arab nationalism**. This concept was rooted in the feeling of sharing the same language, Arabic, and the same religion, Islam (although a tiny minority of Arabs are non-Muslim). But it was more than that because it had a political dimension: the desire for Arab political unity, even to establish a single Arab state. In the First World War, Arab nationalism was boosted by the Arab Revolt of 1916 in which an Arab army fought against the Turks in the Middle East. It was further strengthened, after the war, in opposition to continued European domination: in 1919, British and French mandates were imposed on the Arab countries of Iraq, Syria, Lebanon, Transjordan and Palestine (see page 8).

Above all, however, Arab nationalism emerged as a growing political movement in the 1930s and the main reason was the increasing Jewish immigration to Palestine. Opposition to Zionism was the one issue on which all the Arabs of the Middle East could agree. The events in Palestine, especially the Arab Rebellion from 1936 (see page 13), contributed to the growth of national feeling among Arab people.

Although most Arabs still felt that their first loyalty was to their tribe, clan or region, there was growing support for a single Arab state, especially among the urban, educated classes in countries such as Egypt, Syria, Jordan, Lebanon and Iraq, as well as Palestine. Nevertheless, it was separate Arab states that emerged in the twentieth century and most of their governments did not wish to merge and form a single Arab state. They did, however, show their solidarity when their leaders met in a conference in Cairo in 1945 and formed the Arab League. Then, a few years later, the emergence of the state of Israel and the humiliating defeat of the invading Arab armies united the Arabs in their hatred of the new Jewish state. The Arabs also resented the Western powers, especially Britain and the USA, whom they blamed for the creation of the state of Israel in the first place.

Key date Formation of Arab League: 1945

Nasser and the West

Key question Why did Nasser view the West as a threat?

In Egypt, as we have seen (pages 37–9), it was the war against Israel in 1948–9 that acted as the catalyst that led the army to overthrow the monarchy. Nasser and his fellow army officers had been so appalled by the incompetence of the Egyptian government in the 1948–9 war that they started plotting to take over the government soon afterwards. They overthrew the King's government in 1952. Next, in order to establish complete independence for Egypt, they had to get rid of the British troops who were stationed on the Suez Canal. This they achieved peacefully, by agreement with the British government, in 1954. However, it was also agreed that British officials would continue to operate the Canal and this therefore remained as a symbol of Western domination.

In the 1950s, the British and the Americans tried to persuade Nasser's government to join an anti-Soviet alliance. This was the era of the **Cold War** and the Western powers wished to contain the spread of Soviet power and influence. When the Americans explained to Nasser what a threat Soviet Russia was, he pointed out that it was '5000 miles away'. For him, it was the Western powers and Israel that posed the greater threat to Egypt's stability and independence. Nasser wished to stay independent of any pro-Western alliance. This neutral stand made the Western powers suspicious because they saw things through Cold War eyes: if Egypt was not *for* them, they suspected it must be against them.

Key term **Cold War** A state of tension, but not actual war, that existed between the USA and the Soviet Union between the late 1940s and late 1980s.

Key question
What was the importance of Nasser's campaign against the Baghdad Pact?

Key date

Baghdad Pact formed: 1955

Key term

Baghdad Pact
An alliance formed by Britain, Turkey, Iran and, later, Pakistan and Iraq. Its headquarters were in the Iraqi capital of Baghdad.

The Baghdad Pact 1955

In 1955, at the height of the Cold War, the British formed an anti-Soviet alliance with Turkey and Iran. They tried to persuade the government of Iraq, which was an Arab state, to join. Nasser was furious. He did not want any Arab state to join. It seemed that the British were interfering in Arab affairs again, as they had been doing for much of the twentieth century. Nasser saw the **Baghdad Pact**, as the alliance became known, as an instrument of Western intervention and he feared that Jordan, Lebanon and Syria might also be seduced into joining. That would leave Egypt very isolated. He launched a massive propaganda campaign to prevent Iraq from joining.

'Voice of the Arabs'

To do this, Nasser made use of the Arab world's biggest radio station, the 'Voice of the Arabs', which was broadcast from Cairo and reached millions in the Arab world. Radios were set up in cafés and in village squares. Dozens of people listened to each radio. In this way, Nasser could appeal to the Arab peoples, sometimes against the wishes of their governments. As the radio station declared: 'The Voice of the Arabs speaks for the Arabs, struggles for them and expresses their unity.'

Nasser's main aim was to preserve the power of Egypt but he recognised the wide appeal of Arab nationalism. Through the power of the radio (at a time before television was common) he could strengthen both the power of Egypt and his own leadership of the Arab world. Egypt was the leading Arab state and the strongest military power in the Arab world. Now it had the radio with which to dominate other Arab powers and defy the West.

Cairo radio already had a huge audience throughout the Arab world because Egyptian music was so popular. Egyptian singers (and Egyptian film stars) were famous across the whole of the Middle East. Now the voice of Nasser was also heard by millions and they thrilled to his mesmerising speeches. The Arab masses, particularly in the cities where they had more access to radio, responded with huge enthusiasm. The 'Voice of the Arabs' appealed to Arabs of all classes and across national borders. It went to the heart of Arab politics. In this way, Arab nationalism became an increasingly strong, unifying movement and Nasser was its champion.

Nasser's opposition to what he saw as Western imperialism won so much Arab support that only Iraq, out of all the Arab states, was able to join the Baghdad Pact. Public opinion in Jordan, Lebanon and Syria was swept along by Nasser's oratory and made it impossible for their governments to join the pact. It was Egypt's opposition to any Western alliance that was thus the main contributor to the rise of Arab nationalism in the 1950s.

Nasser and the non-aligned world

As we have seen, Nasser was determined that Egypt should not be drawn into any alliance with the West (or, for that matter, with the Soviet Union). He wanted the Arabs to be neutral and to defend themselves. This neutralist stand won Nasser many admirers beyond the Arab world. The leaders of major countries like India and China admired his independent stance and treated him as an equal. These countries were, like Egypt, determined not to be drawn in to any alliance either with the West or with the Soviet Union. They wanted to keep out of the Cold War and remain **non-aligned**. In 1955, Nasser attended the first conference, in Indonesia, of these non-aligned states. His international prestige grew and he came to be seen as the leader of the whole Arab world.

Nasser and the Suez crisis 1956

Three further events were to accelerate the onward march of Arab nationalism. The first was the so-called Czech arms deal. The second was the Suez crisis of 1956 and the third was the merging of the states of Egypt and Syria in 1958.

The Czech arms deal, September 1955

In September 1955, Nasser announced that he had agreed to buy arms from the Czech government. In return for sales of cotton and rice, Egypt was to be supplied with weapons, including Soviet aircraft and tanks. This was Nasser showing his 'independent' stance which so worried the West. A few months earlier, Israeli armed forces had attacked Egyptian military headquarters in Gaza and killed 35 Egyptian troops. Now, at last, Nasser had secured the weapons Egypt needed to defend itself. The announcement of the Czech arms deal had an electrifying effect, not just in Egypt but in many other Arab countries. On the streets of the Arab cities of Damascus, Amman and Baghdad there was rejoicing. Nasser was seen as a saviour, throwing off the domination of the West and securing the defence of the Arab world. Now at last, the Arabs had achieved their victory over 'imperialism' and its 'illegitimate offspring', Israel.

The Suez crisis, 1956

There was similar euphoria in the Arab world a year later, in 1956, when Britain and France were forced to withdraw from Egypt after attempting to regain control of the Suez Canal. This episode is explained fully on pages 41–4. For a short time, it looked to the Egyptian government as if Cairo might be attacked by Anglo-French forces and Nasser decided to take poison rather than suffer the humiliation of being captured, but then came news that Britain and France were to call off their military action.

Nasser himself recognised that he had been saved by American intervention but, on the radio and throughout the Arab world, it was Egyptian resistance that was portrayed as having won the day. Arab cities erupted in anti-Western demonstrations and riots,

President Nasser waves to the cheering crowd after announcing that he had nationalised the Suez Canal in July 1956.

Key term

Charisma
The capacity to inspire devotion in others, as if endowed with superhuman or, at least, exceptional powers.

Nasser's name was chanted and Arab governments came under huge pressure to bring their policies into line with Egypt. Syria and Saudi Arabia broke off relations with Britain and France while Jordan signed a military pact with Syria and Egypt. In January 1957, a 'Treaty of Arab Solidarity' was signed by Egypt, Syria, Jordan and Saudi Arabia.

Nasser's **charisma**, his perceived victory over Suez and the predominance of Cairo radio contributed to an ever-rising tide of Arab nationalism. This reached its height, in 1958, when Syria demanded a complete merger with Egypt so as to form one state.

Summary diagram: The growth of Arab nationalism

Arab nationalism

Grew in response to Western domination which was shown in:

- mandates in inter-war years
- creation of the state of Israel on Arab land
- continued presence of British troops on Egyptian territory
- pressure to join anti-Soviet alliance such as Baghdad Pact

President Nasser became champion of Arabs in defying the West:

- in his use of Cairo Radio
- in Czech arms deal 1955
- in Suez crisis 1956

2 | The United Arab Republic 1958–61

Some Arab governments, like those of Jordan and Saudi Arabia, remained lukewarm in their attitude towards Nasser's Egypt. Both were ruled by conservative monarchies and were wary of Nasser's radical, even revolutionary politics (see the section on Arab socialism, page 71). When the US government offered aid to countries requesting American help against the threat of **'international communism'**, both Jordan and Saudi Arabia responded and received US aid.

By contrast, Syria accepted economic and military aid from the Soviet Union. The USA was so afraid that Syria might go communist that they persuaded Turkey to move troops to its border with Syria. Nasser unleashed a barrage of propaganda against the USA and its 'reactionary' allies in the Arab world. He also sent a contingent of Egyptian troops to Syria. As a military force, these troops were insignificant but, as a symbol, they had a huge impact on Arab public opinion. Even those leaders who had adopted a pro-American position had to retreat and appear to swim with the Arab nationalist tide. The Syrian parliament went further and voted for immediate union with Egypt!

Syria demands union with Egypt

Nasser was not enthusiastic: Syria had no common border with Egypt and it had completely different political and economic systems. However, Syria's army leaders flew to Cairo and virtually handed their country over to Nasser. The Syrians felt vulnerable: theirs was a small population of just four million. They would feel far more secure if joined to Egypt's 26 million. On the streets of the Syrian capital, Damascus, there was a frenzy demanding the political unity of the 'Arab nation'. Nasser, as the 'hero' of Arab nationalism, was cornered. He insisted that the political and economic systems of Syria would have to be merged with those of Egypt. That would mean Syria closing down its political parties to come into line with one-party Egypt. It would mean bringing its major industries and banks under government control. Yet still the Syrian leaders demanded complete union and, in February 1958, the **United Arab Republic** (UAR) was born.

When Nasser arrived in the Syrian capital at dawn a few weeks later, people poured out of their homes, many still in nightclothes, to welcome him. Nasser made speech after speech to huge crowds. There was dancing, singing of Arab songs and chanting of political slogans. Nasser was treated like a pop or film star. He was, by far, the biggest celebrity in the Arab world. Even in Iraq, Nasser's main Arab rival, big crowds celebrated the news of the new Arab state. Five months later, the Iraqi army overthrew and killed their King and his leading ministers and declared Iraq a **republic**. The country left the Baghdad Pact, which then collapsed. It was widely assumed that Iraq would now join Egypt and Syria and that the three countries, at the heart of the Arab world, would form the bedrock of the Arab nation-state.

Key question
Why did Syria leave
the UAR in 1961?

Key date

Syria left the UAR:
1961

Key term

Coup
Sudden or violent
change of
government.

The end of the UAR 1961

In 1958 Arab nationalism reached the height of its power. But from now onwards, it entered a period of gradual decline. First, the new Iraqi government put its own interests first and decided not to join the UAR. Secondly, the euphoria that had greeted the formation of the UAR soon turned to disillusionment in Syria. There were many reasons, mostly to do with Syrians being made to feel inferior. As expected, the army and the government of the new Arab state were dominated by Egyptians but landowners and businessmen became resentful too. They disliked Nasser's 'Arab socialism' (see the box below). The Egyptians insisted that Syria carry out land reform, breaking up the big estates and redistributing land to the peasants, as had been done in Egypt. Then the major industries and the banks in Syria were taken over by the government. What may have worked in Egypt did not go down well in Syria. The urban masses may have remained loyal to the UAR but the élites became disaffected. In September 1961 Syrian army officers carried out a **coup** against those 'who have humiliated Syria and degraded her army'. Egyptian forces did not intervene and the new Syrian Prime Minister said he wanted to maintain a close alliance with Egypt: there was still huge support among Syrians for the idea of Arab unity. But Nasser's prestige and his status as the unifying symbol of Arab nationalism were dented.

Nasser's 'Arab socialism'

After coming to power, Nasser had set out to transform the Egyptian economy and share the country's wealth more fairly. He started with land reform. In the early 1950s, a small number of landowners owned a third of the cultivated land in Egypt while 72 per cent of the rural population owned an acre or less. Nasser's government passed a law which limited land owning to 200 acres per person, later reduced to 100 acres. The land confiscated from those who owned more than this amount was then redistributed amongst the poorer farmers.

Later, in 1961, the government nationalised the export of cotton, Egypt's main product, and took over the banks and many large industrial companies. They also confiscated the property of over a thousand of the wealthiest landowners. This huge programme, accompanied by an expansion in schools and hospitals, was intended to reduce poverty and increase opportunities for the masses. By the mid-1960s most Egyptians were considerably better off, certainly healthier and better fed, than they had been when Nasser came to power. They had also regained pride and dignity after years of foreign domination.

Yemen 1962

In 1962 a group of pro-Egyptian army officers seized power in the small, poor Arab state of Yemen, which borders Saudi Arabia (see the map on page 1). The son of the deposed monarch escaped to the mountains and gained the support of the tribesmen. He also secured aid from the Saudi government. The army officers declared Yemen a republic and sought Nasser's aid. Nasser thought such aid would be required only on a small scale and for a short period of time. Yet, by 1965, he had 70,000 troops there and only finally withdrew, having got bogged down in a guerrilla war, in 1967. As he later admitted: it was 'a miscalculation: we never thought it would lead to what it did'.

Nasser, the Arabs and Israel 1963–7

Despite these setbacks, Nasser was still a towering figure in the Arab world and the best-known Arab leader on the international stage. In 1963 there were further military coups in both Syria and Iraq and the new governments looked to Nasser to form a 'new movement of Arab unity'. The plans came to nothing but Nasser saw the need for joint Arab action to face a new threat from Israel. The Israelis were about to complete a project to divert 75 per cent of the water from the River Jordan to Israel for irrigation and industrial development. This was seen as a great threat to Syria and Jordan, both of which depended on water from the river.

Nasser presented the Israeli project as an act of aggression and a challenge to the whole Arab world, not just to Syria and Jordan which would be most affected. The young hotheads in the new Syrian government talked of taking military action but Nasser knew the Arab states were not prepared for war and that Israel had far stronger military forces. So he called for a conference of Arab leaders in Cairo in January 1964. This was attended by kings and presidents, allies and rivals, all united in opposition to Israel. At the conference, the leaders agreed to set up the Palestine Liberation Organisation (PLO) to represent the Palestinian people in the struggle for the 'liberation of Palestine'. In effect, the Arab leaders had postponed the issue of how to deal with the Israeli threat but had put on a show of solidarity.

Over the next three years the Syrian government actively supported the PLO in launching guerrilla raids into Israel. Nasser did not yet want war with Israel because many of his forces were involved in Yemen. Besides, he knew that Israel was a stronger military power than Syria and Egypt combined. Yet he felt drawn to support radical, Arab nationalists, especially in the struggle with Israel. In August 1966, the Egyptian government announced: 'Damascus [the capital of Syria] does not stand alone against imperialist plots.'

Egypt then signed a defence agreement with Syria which stated that aggression against either state would be considered an attack on the other. Nasser rose again as the outstanding champion of the Arab cause. But the agreement with Syria paved the way for the chain of events that led to a disastrous war for the Arab states of Egypt, Syria and Jordan. This war, in 1967, which is known as the Six-Day War, was examined in Chapter 3.

Key question
Why did Nasser hold a conference of Arab leaders in 1964?

Nasser sent military aid to the Yemen: 1962–7

Conference of Arab leaders in Cairo: 1964

Formation of the Palestine Liberation Organisation (PLO): 1964

Six-Day War: 1967

Key dates

Profile: Gamal Abdul Nasser 1918–70

1918	– Born in Alexandria, in Egypt, the son of a postman
1938	– Graduated as an officer from the military academy
1948	– Fought in the first Arab–Israeli War
1949	– Became a founder of the Free Officers' Movement
1952	– Led the military coup that overthrew the Egyptian monarchy
1954–70	– President of Egypt

Nasser came from a modest background but was able to gain admission to the Egyptian Military Academy. Like several of his fellow young army officers, he was shocked by defeat against Israel in 1948–9 and appalled by the incompetence of King Farouk's government. He led the coup that overthrew the King in 1952 and became leader of the new republican government in Egypt. He set out to strengthen the country and make it completely independent. This meant building up the armed forces and securing the withdrawal of British troops. He achieved this peacefully, but his nationalisation of the Suez Canal provoked an invasion by British, French and Israeli forces. Nevertheless, the British and French were forced to withdraw. Nasser thus emerged as the victor and won fame throughout the Arab world for his defiance of the European powers.

Nasser became the undisputed leader of the Arab world, winning popular support on a scale never achieved before or since by any Arab leader. His speeches, broadcast on Cairo radio, drew millions of listeners and their effect on popular opinion was such that governments in other Arab were often forced to follow Nasser's line. In 1958, the Syrian leaders virtually begged Nasser to join Syria and Egypt together to form the United Arab Republic. Although this union was greeted with euphoria at the start, it only lasted three years. Despite this setback, Nasser's popularity and prestige in the Arab world remained unrivalled for several more years.

Defeat at the hands of the Israelis in 1967 was a heavy blow. The Egyptian armed forces were humiliated, Sinai was lost and the Suez Canal remained closed for several years as the Israelis were encamped on the eastern bank (see page 54). Exhausted, Nasser died of a heart attack in 1970. He was mourned by millions throughout the Arab world.

The death of Nasser 1970

Key date

Death of Nasser: 1970

On the third evening of the Six-Day War in 1967, with the Egyptian air force smashed and the army in retreat, Nasser announced that he would resign. Public opinion demanded that he stay. He was well loved, as well as a very dominant leader, and would not be allowed to leave office in the midst of crisis. Nevertheless, Egypt's defeat in the war was a humiliation for Nasser and for the whole Arab world. Although Egypt's army and air force were replenished by Soviet weapons, Egypt was severely weakened. Nasser never fully recovered from the shock of the war and, in 1970, he died, aged 52, from a heart attack.

Nasser had brought unity to the Arab world and, although his influence was declining before he died, it was only after his death that the underlying divisions amongst the Arab states came to the surface and revealed how fragmented the Arab world had become.

Postscript: Anwar Sadat

Nasser's successor as President of Egypt was Anwar Sadat. He adopted a very different approach in his relations with Israel and the West. He went to war with Israel in 1973 (see page 55) but, afterwards, he sought US help in order to make peace with Israel. In recognising the state of Israel, he became, in the eyes of most of the Arab world, a traitor to the cause of Arab nationalism. This is dealt with more fully on pages 58–9.

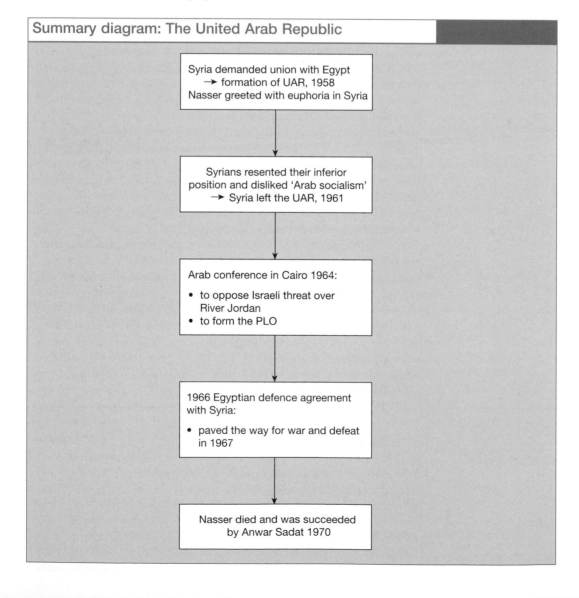

Summary diagram: The United Arab Republic

Syria demanded union with Egypt → formation of UAR, 1958
Nasser greeted with euphoria in Syria

↓

Syrians resented their inferior position and disliked 'Arab socialism' → Syria left the UAR, 1961

↓

Arab conference in Cairo 1964:
- to oppose Israeli threat over River Jordan
- to form the PLO

↓

1966 Egyptian defence agreement with Syria:
- paved the way for war and defeat in 1967

↓

Nasser died and was succeeded by Anwar Sadat 1970

Study Guide

In the style of Edexcel and OCR

How far do you agree that it was the creation of the state of Israel that fuelled the growth of Arab nationalism during the years 1948–73?

Exam tips

The cross-references are intended to take you straight to the material that will help you to answer the question.

First, read Chapter 4 again.

In this essay, you have to assess the degree to which the creation of Israel was a factor in developing and sustaining Arab nationalism. To answer the question of 'How far?' and thus achieve a high grade, you need to examine the importance of the state of Israel in the context of other influencing factors.

First, you might explain briefly what you mean by 'Arab nationalism' (page 65). Then, in examining the importance of the existence of Israel, you should consider:

- how the UN decision to create the new state united the Arab world and contributed to the invasion by Arab armies in May 1948 (pages 20–2)
- how the defeat of Arab armies increased hatred of Israel and, for the next 25 years, the one thing that united the Arab world was its refusal to recognise the new state
- the formation of the PLO, in order to liberate Palestine and destroy Israel, helped to sustain Arab nationalism
- the importance of the 1967 and 1973 wars in strengthening anti-Israeli and pro-Arab nationalist feelings (pages 52–7).

You will also need to examine the role of Egypt, especially President Nasser, in fuelling Arab nationalism. In particular, you should explain his defiance of the West, as shown in:

- Nasser's use of the radio in building opposition, throughout the Arab world, to the Baghdad Pact (page 67)
- Egypt's 'victory' over the West (specifically Britain and France) in the Suez War, 1956 (pages 68–9)
- the formation of the UAR, again strengthening feelings of Arab nationalism (page 70).

The best answers will show the links between Israel's existence and other factors fuelling Arab nationalism. For example, much Arab nationalism was essentially anti-Western, especially in its opposition to what was seen as the West's creation of, and continuing support for, the state of Israel. The Suez crisis of 1956 shows this most clearly: it was portrayed, throughout the Arab world, as aggression by Western 'imperialists' and their 'illegitimate offspring', Israel.

Be sure to provide a clear and strong conclusion that answers the question. Do not sit on the fence.

5 The Palestinian Problem

POINTS TO CONSIDER
This chapter will focus on the Palestinian problem: the problem of a people without a home. It will examine the plight of the refugees and the rise of the PLO. It will show how PLO military activities led to the Israeli invasion of Lebanon and, finally, it will study the origins and impact of the Palestinian *Intifada* (uprising). These developments are covered under the following headings:

- The Palestine Liberation Organisation
- War in Lebanon
- The Palestinian *Intifada* 1987–93

Key dates

1959	Fatah set up
1964	Formation of the PLO
1967	Six-Day War
1968	The 'Battle of Karameh'
1969	Arafat became Chairman of the PLO
1970	PLO expelled from Jordan
1972	Israeli athletes killed at the Olympic Games
1978 and 1982	Israeli invasions of Lebanon
1987–93	Palestinian *Intifada*

1 | The Palestine Liberation Organisation

The Palestinian refugees

During the fighting between Israel and the Arabs in 1948–9, over 700,000 Arabs fled from their homes in Palestine. As you can see on the map on page 77, most of them went to the West Bank or the Gaza Strip. Large numbers also went to Syria, Jordan and Lebanon. Today the UN reckons there are about four million Palestinian refugees.

After the war ended in 1949 the UN formed the UN Relief and Works Agency (UNRWA). This body set up camps for the refugees and provided food, clothing, shelter and education. At first, the refugees lived in tents, later in huts made of mud, corrugated iron or concrete. The camps became the shanty towns of the

Key question
What were conditions like in the refugee camps?

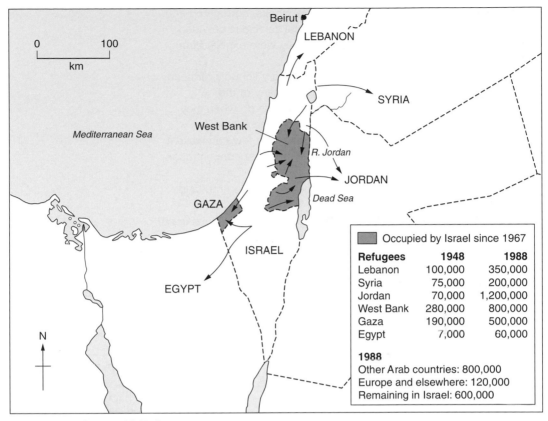

Refugees	1948	1988
Lebanon	100,000	350,000
Syria	75,000	200,000
Jordan	70,000	1,200,000
West Bank	280,000	800,000
Gaza	190,000	500,000
Egypt	7,000	60,000

1988
Other Arab countries: 800,000
Europe and elsewhere: 120,000
Remaining in Israel: 600,000

Palestinian refugees 1948–9.

Middle East. The conditions are described below, first by a British observer, then by a refugee and, finally, by a UN official:

> The conditions in the camps were atrocious. Families huddled bleakly in overcrowded tents. They were without adequate food or sanitation. When it rained, the narrow paths along each row were churned into mud which oozed into the tents. They lived in sodden clothes and slept in wet blankets. Influenza reached epidemic proportions. The young and old perished. Malnourished children were too weak to resist, and the old, left with no purpose, lacked the will.
>
> (Jonathan Dimbleby, a British observer, comments in
> *The Palestinians*, 1979)

> A few months after our arrival, we were penniless and had to move into a refugee camp with 2000 other homeless Palestinians. It is beyond human endurance for a family of 11 to live in a small tent through all the seasons of the year on UNRWA rations. Fathers buried their children who died of hunger. Some buried their fathers who died of disease. On winter days we all crawled together to gain the warmth of humans.
>
> (Ghazi Daniel, a refugee remembers, in an account published by
> the PLO, 1972)

They live in little huts of mud and concrete blocks, corrugated iron roofs, row after row. Fairly adequate medical service is provided, probably better than was enjoyed before they were expelled from their native villages.

Children swarm everywhere. There are primary schools for nearly all of them. There are secondary schools for many of the adolescents. And what will these youths and girls do when they have finished their secondary school training? There is no employment for them in the [Gaza] Strip, and very few can leave it to work elsewhere. The Gaza Strip resembles a vast concentration camp.

They can look to the east and see wide fields, once Arab land, cultivated extensively by a few Israelis.

(General Burns, a UN Commander, describes the conditions in the camps in Gaza in the 1950s)

The plight of the refugees

The UN wished to **repatriate** the refugees, but the Israelis refused to allow them to return to their lands in Israel. Instead, the Israelis continued to take over Arab villages and to confiscate the property of Palestinians who had fled from Israel. Much of this 'absentee property' was given to new Jewish immigrants. The Israeli 'Law of Return' allows any Jew anywhere in the world to go and live in Israel but forbids Palestinians to do so.

Key question
Was there a solution to the refugee problem?

Repatriate
To send people back to their own country.

Key term

A refugee camp in Jordan 1949. Of which of the conditions described in the extracts on pages 77–8 can you see evidence in the photograph?

An Israeli politician later explained on US television:

> We want to have a Jewish state. We can absorb the Arabs, but then it won't be the same country. We want a Jewish state like the French have a French state.

By 1953 Israel had absorbed 300,000 Jews from Arab countries and insisted that those same Arab countries should find homes for the Palestinian refugees. Jordan allowed the Palestinian refugees to settle and become citizens of Jordan but other Arab states kept them in refugee camps near the borders with Israel. Most of the refugees themselves dreamt of 'the Return': they were Palestinians and they wanted to return to their homes in Palestine.

Some Palestinians migrated to other parts of the Middle East or the West. They became engineers, teachers, doctors or businessmen. A small number became very wealthy. But the vast majority of the refugees remained poor and unemployed. In their camps, they formed a ring of human misery round the borders of Israel. Crowded together, they became frustrated and bitter. It was from the camps that the Palestine Liberation Organisation (PLO) recruited most of its members.

Key dates

Fatah set up: 1959

Formation of the PLO: 1964

Six-Day War: 1967

The origins of the PLO

Since the end of the first Arab–Israeli war in 1949, Palestinians had been crossing the border into Israel, often just to try and retrieve their property. Later, some of them carried out armed raids, sometimes killing the new Jewish 'owners' of their property. The Israeli Defence Force (IDF) retaliated forcefully. In 1959 a new group of Palestinian fighters emerged. Its name was Fatah, which comes from the Arabic initials of its name 'The Movement for the Liberation of Palestine'. When spelt backwards, the initials spell *fatah*, which is the Arabic word for 'victory'. Fatah's leader was Yasser Arafat and its goal was to create a Palestinian state.

Key term

Palestine Liberation Organisation (PLO)
As well as leading the armed struggle to regain Palestine, the PLO provided many health and welfare services in the Palestinian refugee camps. The Red Crescent society, which set up and ran hospitals, was headed by Yasser Arafat's brother.

Five years later, in 1964, the **Palestine Liberation Organisation (PLO)** was set up by Arab leaders meeting in Cairo (see page 72). The aim of the PLO was to unite all Palestinians in the struggle to win back their land. The largest group within the PLO was Fatah. From 1965 to 1967, Fatah carried out an increasing number of guerrilla attacks on Israel and was supported by the Arab states which bordered Israel, especially Syria. However, after the Six-Day War of 1967, things were to be very different for Fatah and the PLO as a whole.

Key question
Why was the Six-Day War a turning point for the Palestinians?

The impact of the Six-Day War 1967

Syria, Jordan and Egypt, which had provided vital support for the PLO, were weakened by their heavy losses in the war. At the same time, Egypt and Syria became far more concerned about the lands they had lost to Israel than about the Palestinian refugees. Many Palestinians were now convinced that they would have to fight for their homeland on their own. This was even more urgent now that all the original land of Palestine, including the West Bank and Gaza Strip, was under Israeli rule.

Over 350,000 Palestinians fled from the West Bank when it was captured by the Israelis in 1967. Most of the refugees went to Jordan. In fact, from 1967, half the population of Jordan was Palestinian. Fatah and other groups within the PLO now concentrated their forces in Jordan and started to recruit far more volunteers from the refugee camps. Ghazi Daniel was one of many Palestinian refugees for whom 1967 was a turning point:

> The aggressive war of 1967 was a landmark in my life. The new expansion of Israel and the new waves of refugees multiplied the tragedy many times. This is why I have joined the Palestine Liberation Movement. We shall fight for the Palestinians' return.

Fatah increased its raids into Israel. Its guerrilla forces planted bombs and mines, and attacked military installations. In retaliation, in 1968, the Israelis crossed the border into Jordan and launched a full-scale attack on a major Fatah base in Karameh. The Israelis had 15,000 troops as well as tanks and planes. The Palestinians had 300 fighters. Although the Israelis destroyed the Palestinian base, the Palestinian forces, with the aid of Jordanian troops, knocked out several Israeli tanks and planes and killed 28 Israeli troops. They had proved that the Israelis were not invincible. This inspired thousands of Arabs, not just Palestinians, to join the Palestinian guerrillas: in fact, 5000 enlisted in the next two days. Between 1967 and 1970 Fatah forces killed over 500 Israelis. This was almost as many as the Israelis had lost in the whole Six-Day War.

Key dates

The 'Battle of Karameh': 1968

Arafat became Chairman of the PLO: 1969

Arafat becomes leader of the PLO

In 1968 the Palestinian fighters, led by Fatah, gained control of the PLO and, in 1969, Yasser Arafat, now internationally known as a result of the battle of Karameh, became Chairman. The new charter of the PLO proclaimed: 'Armed struggle is the only way to liberate Palestine'. Arafat tried to co-ordinate the guerrilla

Key question
Why did some Palestinian groups disagree with Arafat's methods?

Yasser Arafat was born in Jerusalem in 1929. He was one of the founders of the Fatah organisation and became chairman of the PLO in 1969. For reasons of security, he slept in a different bed every night.

Key term

Palestinian Front for the Liberation of Palestine (PFLP) An organisation set up by George Habash, a Palestinian Christian. It carried out many terrorist acts.

activities of the various groups within the PLO. Like most of the PLO leaders, he wanted to limit the raids and the bombings to Israeli territory and Israeli targets because their military aim was strictly war on Israel. However, some more radical Palestinian groups, such as the **Palestinian Front for the Liberation of Palestine (PFLP)**, started to carry out attacks in other parts of the world. They pointed out that raids into Israel had achieved very little. They were impatient. They were not prepared to wait 10 or 20 years to regain their country. Some of their views are shown on page 82.

Hijacks and hostages

Key question
What terrorist attacks were carried out?

In December 1968 two Palestinians, members of the PFLP, hijacked an Israeli passenger plane at Athens airport in Greece, killing one man. The Israelis retaliated by destroying 13 aircraft in an attack on Beirut airport in Lebanon, which is where the hijackers had come from. In the following years there were many hijackings, kidnappings and bombings in Europe and elsewhere. At first the targets were Israeli planes, embassies and offices but, in February 1970, a Swiss plane was blown up on its way to Israel. The Israelis usually responded to these attacks by bombing Palestinian bases in Lebanon, Jordan and Syria. Often these bases were near refugee camps so that hundreds of innocent Palestinians died. These Israeli reprisals received far less publicity in the Western press than the Palestinian attacks.

The PLO are expelled from Jordan 1970

Key question
Why was the PLO expelled from Jordan?

Key date
PLO expelled from Jordan: 1970

Sometimes terrorist violence led Arab to fight Arab. In Jordan, King Hussein feared the Israeli reprisals which followed Palestinian attacks that were launched from his country. In 1968 his troops had helped the Palestinians to inflict heavy casualties on the Israelis at Karameh. However, in September 1970, he decided he did not want any more raids launched on Israel from inside Jordan. Besides, members of the PLO were acting as if they ruled much of Jordan, not just the refugee camps: they were roaming round fully armed and setting up road blocks, even in Amman, the Jordanian capital. So he ordered the Palestinians to obey him and his army.

Then, in the same month, four aircraft were hijacked by the PFLP and three of the planes (belonging to British, Swiss and American airlines) were taken to a Palestinian base in Jordan. The hijackers demanded the release of Palestinian fighters held in British, German and Swiss, as well as Israeli, jails. The passengers were set free but the British plane was blown up. This incident was the last straw for King Hussein. It was a direct challenge to his authority and he feared foreign intervention. He was forced to act. He ordered his army to take control of the PLO bases. The Palestinians resisted and, in the next 10 days, more than 3000 of them were killed. The PLO offices in Jordan were shut down and their newspapers banned. The remaining fighters went to Syria and Lebanon.

Black September

Palestinian extremists later got their revenge by murdering the Jordanian Prime Minister while he was in Egypt. The killers were members of a group called **Black September**, named after the month in which the Palestinian bases in Jordan were wiped out. Soon they began sending letter bombs to Israeli embassies in Europe.

Then, on 5 September 1972, they stunned the whole world. They attacked the Israeli athletes who were competing in the Olympic Games in Germany. They killed two athletes and then demanded the release of 200 Palestinian prisoners in Israel. When German police attempted a rescue, the Palestinians killed nine more athletes. The Palestinians got the massive publicity they wanted for their cause but not the release of their comrades. A few days later the Israelis took their revenge and carried out reprisal raids on Syria and Lebanon, in which over 200 refugees were killed.

Black September
A Palestinian group which killed 11 Israeli athletes at the 1972 Olympics.

Key term

Israeli athletes killed at the Olympic Games: 1972

Key date

The effects on world opinion

Acts of terrorism made the Palestinians unpopular in the rest of the world. People were shocked by such brutal deeds. They branded the PLO, as a whole, as terrorists. However, terrorist acts made many people in Europe and other parts of the world begin to think more about the Palestinian problem. They read about the crowded, unhealthy camps in which hundreds of thousands of refugees had lived for 20 years. They came to understand that the Palestinian people were the helpless victims of war and asked themselves whether the guerrillas were in fact terrorists or freedom fighters.

Key question
What did the PLO achieve by using terrorism?

Terrorists or freedom fighters?

What reasons are given for the use of violence by each of the Palestinians quoted below?

George Habash, leader of the PFLP, said:

> When we hijack a plane it has more effect than if we killed 100 Israelis in battle. For decades world public opinion has been neither for nor against the Palestinians. It simply ignored us. At least the world is talking about us now.

In the early 1970s, Sami el-Karami, a Palestinian, said:

> The non-violent methods are very beautiful and very easy, and we wish we could win with these methods. Our people do not carry machine guns and bombs because they enjoy killing. It is for us the last resort. For 22 years we have waited for the United Nations and the United States, for liberty, for freedom and democracy. There was no result. So this is our last resort.

A Palestinian student in Lebanon wrote to his parents in 1968:

> For 20 years our people have been waiting for a just solution to the Palestinian problem. All that we got was charity and humiliation

while others continue to live in our homes. I refuse to remain a refugee. I have decided to join the freedom fighters and I ask for your blessing.

A Palestinian woman, quoted in *The Middle East*, by Walter Oppenheim, explained:

I am proud that my son did not die in this refugee camp. The foreign press come here and take pictures of us standing in queues to obtain food rations. This is no life. I am proud that my son died in action, fighting on our occupied soil. I am already preparing my eight-year-old for the day he can fight for freedom too.

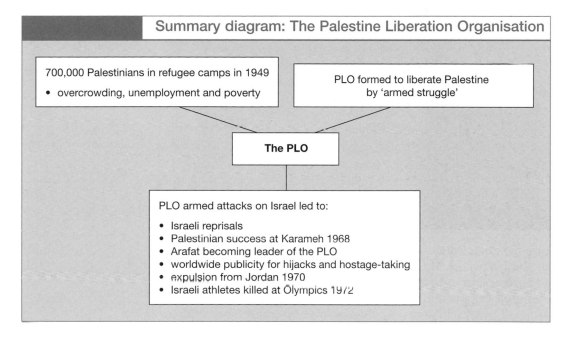

Summary diagram: The Palestine Liberation Organisation

700,000 Palestinians in refugee camps in 1949
- overcrowding, unemployment and poverty

PLO formed to liberate Palestine by 'armed struggle'

The PLO

PLO armed attacks on Israel led to:
- Israeli reprisals
- Palestinian success at Karameh 1968
- Arafat becoming leader of the PLO
- worldwide publicity for hijacks and hostage-taking
- expulsion from Jordan 1970
- Israeli athletes killed at Olympics 1972

2 | War in Lebanon

On 10 April 1985 a 16-year-old Muslim girl, Sana M'Heidli, set off on a special mission. She drove a car packed with explosives towards a group of Israeli soldiers in Lebanon and then detonated the charge. She killed herself and two Israelis. We know it was a suicide mission because she explained what she was going to do on video beforehand. The photograph on the next page comes from the video. It was later shown on television in Lebanon.

Key question
Why did the Israelis invade Lebanon in 1978 and 1982?

Crisis in Lebanon

Until the 1970s Lebanon was a fairly stable country and its capital, Beirut, was one of the richest cities in the Middle East. Most of the population were either Christian or Muslim, although both groups were made up of several different sects. Since 1943, they had kept to the agreement that the President would be a Christian and the Prime Minister a Muslim and just over half the

Sana M'Heidli, 16-year-old suicide bomber. In her pre-recorded videotape, she said: 'I chose death in order to fulfil my national duty.' What drove her to this desperate act? What were Israeli troops doing in Lebanon anyway?

posts in government would go to the Christian majority. However, by the 1970s, the Muslim population had overtaken the Christians and were demanding more power.

A more significant source of instability was the Palestinians. Many of them had come as refugees in 1948–9 and more of them arrived after the Six-Day War of 1967. However, the most destabilising force of all was the PLO whose armed forces had set up more bases in Lebanon after they were expelled from Jordan in 1970 (see page 81). Soon they came to dominate southern Lebanon (some called it 'Fatahland') and frequently bombed Jewish settlements and villages in the Galilee region of northern Israel (see map on page 25). The Israelis hit back and, when they did so, Lebanese as well as Palestinians were killed.

In 1975 the Lebanese government ordered its army to regain control of the south. The Palestinians resisted and were helped by Lebanese Muslims. Most of the Lebanese army were Christian and soon there was a civil war between Christians and Muslims. Meanwhile, the PLO continued to carry out attacks on Israel from Lebanon. In 1978 a PLO suicide squad went further south and attacked a bus near Tel Aviv, killing 37 passengers.

Three days after the bus bombing, Israeli troops invaded Lebanon. They seized the south of the country but the PLO forces melted away. The Israelis withdrew, under pressure from the USA, and UN troops were sent to keep the peace on the Lebanese–Israeli border. Over the next four years, the Palestinian armed forces grew in strength. Lebanon had become the main focus of their military operations against Israel and they received a constant stream of recruits from the 400,000 Palestinians in the refugee camps in Lebanon.

'Operation Peace for Galilee' 1982

Key date

Israeli invasions of Lebanon: 1978 and 1982

In the early months of 1982 the Israelis planned another invasion of Lebanon, to be called 'Operation Peace for Galilee'. They simply needed a pretext. This came in June 1982 when a group of Palestinians attempted to murder the Israeli ambassador in London. Those responsible were extremists, opposed to Yasser Arafat, but that made no difference to the Israelis. This was the trigger they needed. Israeli forces again rolled across the Lebanese border. This time they had 170,000 troops, 3500 tanks and 600 fighter planes. The UN peacekeeping forces were powerless to stop them. The Israelis were more successful in destroying PLO forces than they had been in 1978. However, thousands of Palestinian and Lebanese civilians were killed in the process and hundreds of thousands were made homeless.

The Israeli Minister of Defence, Ariel Sharon, told the Israeli Prime Minister and his cabinet that the aim was to drive out the Palestinian forces, destroy their bases and establish a 40-km security zone in southern Lebanon in order to protect the Israelis living in Galilee. However, it soon became obvious that Sharon was far more ambitious because the Israelis advanced north and surrounded the capital, Beirut (see the map on page 77). They cut off supplies of food and water. They started shelling positions in the city which were held by the PLO. These positions were often in crowded residential areas so thousands more civilians were killed. As well as encircling Beirut on land, the Israelis had complete control of the sky and the coastline. Beirut was bombarded daily, from air, land and sea, for two months. On one day alone in August 1982 there were 127 air raids launched on the city. Over 20,000 people were killed and many more wounded during the 'Battle of Beirut'.

The evacuation of the PLO

Key question
How was the siege of Baghdad ended?

Eventually, in mid-August, the USA intervened. The Americans persuaded the Israelis to stop shelling the city in return for an agreement that the PLO fighters would be evacuated. US, French and Italian troops were sent out to supervise the evacuation. Over 14,000 Palestinian fighters left Beirut to travel to other Arab states. Yasser Arafat, the last to leave, moved his headquarters to Tunisia.

The Americans had assured Arafat that Palestinian civilians would not be harmed after the PLO forces left Beirut. However, the Israelis believed that there were still 2000 Palestinian fighters left in the refugee camps of Sabra and Shatila in Beirut. When on 14 September the newly elected Christian President of Lebanon was killed, his armed supporters took their revenge. They invaded the refugee camps and, over the next two days, they carried out a massacre of men, women and children. The Israeli troops were ordered to let them in and not to intervene. They just stood by. Investigators later reckoned that between 1000 and 2000 people were killed. The rest of the world was horrified. Even in Israel, a crowd of 400,000 protested against the actions of their armed forces. An Israeli government inquiry later blamed Sharon and said he was unfit to be Defence Minister. He was forced to resign although this did not prevent his becoming Prime Minister in 2001.

The Israelis withdraw 1985

After the PLO forces left Beirut, the Israelis withdrew their troops from the capital but they stayed in the south of Lebanon. They had succeeded in driving out the Palestinian armed forces although they could still not be sure that they had driven them *all* out: the guerrillas could easily hide in the huge, crowded refugee camps in southern Lebanon. Worse still, the Israelis had made many enemies amongst the Lebanese, especially the Muslims, in the south. Many of these were to become members of **Hizbollah**, a fiercely anti-Israeli organisation.

The Israeli government faced further problems. International opinion blamed them for thousands of civilian deaths while, in Israel itself, huge numbers demonstrated against the war. They accused the government of turning a defensive war into an aggressive one and of sending hundreds of Israelis, as well as thousands of Palestinians and Lebanese, to their deaths unnecessarily.

Over the next two years, there were regular assaults on Israeli troops in the south of Lebanon. When Israelis heard news of events like Sana M'Heidli's attack on their troops (see page 83), many of them demanded a complete withdrawal from Lebanon. In 1985, Israeli troops withdrew from most of Lebanon, leaving only a small military presence in the 'security zone' along the southern border. This was the longest war Israel had fought. Many regarded it as its first defeat.

Key question
What had the Israelis achieved?

Hizbollah
A radical Islamic group based in southern Lebanon.

Key term

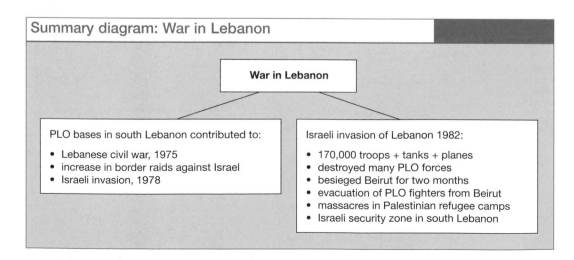

Summary diagram: War in Lebanon

War in Lebanon

PLO bases in south Lebanon contributed to:
- Lebanese civil war, 1975
- increase in border raids against Israel
- Israeli invasion, 1978

Israeli invasion of Lebanon 1982:
- 170,000 troops + tanks + planes
- destroyed many PLO forces
- besieged Beirut for two months
- evacuation of PLO fighters from Beirut
- massacres in Palestinian refugee camps
- Israeli security zone in south Lebanon

Key question
Why did a Palestinian uprising break out in the occupied territories in 1987?

Key date

Palestinian *Intifada*: 1987–93

Key term

Intifada
The Palestinian uprising that erupted in Gaza and the West Bank in 1987.

3 | The Palestinian *Intifada* 1987–93

On 8 December 1987 an Israeli army vehicle in Gaza crashed into a lorry, killing four of the Palestinians on board. Rumours spread that it had been a deliberate act of revenge for the killing of an Israeli two days before. The funerals of the Palestinians became huge demonstrations. At one of them a youth was shot dead by an Israeli soldier. As tension mounted, thousands of Palestinians took to the streets, both in Gaza and on the West Bank, and put up barricades of tyres and corrugated iron. From behind them, they stoned Israeli army patrols. The crash that killed four Palestinians sparked off the *Intifada*, or uprising. What were the roots of this uprising?

Life in the occupied territories

Since the Six-Day War of 1967, thousands of Israeli troops had been stationed in Gaza and the West Bank. For many Israelis, the West Bank was vital to Israel's security; it protected the country's narrow waist (it is only 24 km from the Mediterranean to the West Bank). If Israel held on to these lands, they would be finishing off the job they had started in 1948–9 by securing control of the rest of Palestine.

In the end, Israel never actually annexed Gaza and the West Bank. The two areas never became part of the state of Israel with all the inhabitants becoming Israeli citizens. Instead, they became known as the 'occupied territories' and the occupying force was the Israeli army. Military rule was imposed. Resistance was dealt with harshly and was interpreted in many ways: holding a rally or demonstration, organising a strike or just waving the Palestinian flag. Israeli troops rounded up PLO suspects and others whom they saw as a threat to their security. Thousands were jailed without trial, some tortured and hundreds were deported (usually to Jordan). Sometimes their houses were blown up, leaving their families homeless.

The Israeli army also confiscated land and declared it to be Jewish property. This was sometimes done for security reasons, to keep an eye on the Palestinians. However, much of this land was allocated for the building of Jewish settlements and thousands of Jewish civilians were given financial incentives to move to these settlements. The Israeli military authorities also built roads, to link the towns and settlements, and established military camps and checkpoints. The movement of Palestinians was closely monitored and they were regularly stopped at road blocks.

There was another reason for building Jewish settlements: for many Israelis, the West Bank is known as Judea and Samaria, part of the ancient land of Israel, the land that God had promised to the Israelites. Many of the Jewish settlers were determined to colonise this land so that it could never be given back to the Palestinians. It was part of Eretz Israel, the Israel of the Bible.

It became a common sight for the Palestinians to see Jewish settlements being built on land they considered to be theirs. By 1987, there were over 80,000 Israelis living in settlements in and

Young Palestinians hurl stones at Israeli soldiers in Gaza in 1987.

around Jerusalem and another 20,000 living in parts of the West Bank and in Gaza. The *Intifada* may have been triggered by a single incident but years of living under Israeli occupation, with all its daily humiliations, had brought the increasing hatred and tension to boiling point.

The outbreak of the *Intifada* 1987

The *Intifada* took everyone by surprise: Israel, the PLO, the Arab states and the rest of the world. It was spontaneous and completely unplanned. At first, it mainly consisted of people setting up barricades and throwing stones at Israeli troops. But soon it took the form of huge demonstrations and strikes. It involved children as well as adults, women as well as men, labourers as well as businessmen, villagers as well as townspeople, refugees from the camps as well as shopkeepers. It became a national uprising.

The Israeli response and its effects

Not surprisingly, the Israeli government insisted on an 'iron-fist' policy: their troops used tear gas, water cannons, rubber bullets, even live ammunition. But they could not halt the momentum of the uprising. Newspapers and television around the world showed teenagers being shot by Israeli troops. This led the Israeli government to announce that it would no longer use bullets. Instead, they adopted a policy of 'might, force and beatings'. There were mass arrests and special detention camps were set up. Those thought to be leading the uprising were deported or even assassinated. But there was no end to the *Intifada* and the death rate kept rising. By September 1988, 346 Palestinians had been killed. Many of them were under 16 years of age.

Key question
What was the Israeli response?

Worldwide publicity was given to the tear-gassing of demonstrators, the beatings of men, women and children, the closing of schools and colleges. The world saw a powerful, modern army let loose against civilians who were fighting for their human rights and the right to govern themselves.

In Israel itself, opinion was divided: some demanded the use of greater force, others recognised that the *Intifada* was a genuinely popular rising and that it could not be put down by military means. An Israeli professor said:

> An army can beat an army, but an army cannot beat a people. Israel is learning that power has limits. Iron can smash iron, it cannot smash an unarmed fist.

Moves towards a peaceful solution

Many Israelis came to see that the *Intifada* was a war that could not be won: some of them believed that there had to be a political solution. Many Palestinians in Gaza and the West Bank came to the same conclusion. The *Intifada* raised their morale and boosted their confidence but it did not improve their miserable living conditions or end the occupation. Palestinian leaders in Gaza and the West Bank realised they had to put pressure on the PLO leaders in Tunisia to recognise Israel and to persuade the Israeli government to accept a Palestinian state.

The role of the USA, Israel's main ally, was crucial. There was much sympathy in America for the Palestinians and many Jewish Americans began to question the methods used by the Israeli forces. The key breakthrough came late in 1988 when the US government recognised the PLO as a necessary partner in any peace negotiations. Up until this time, the USA had refused to have any dealings with the PLO but, when the PLO leaders showed willing to recognise the state of Israel, the Americans changed their policy. The way was now open for the start of what became known as the 'peace process'.

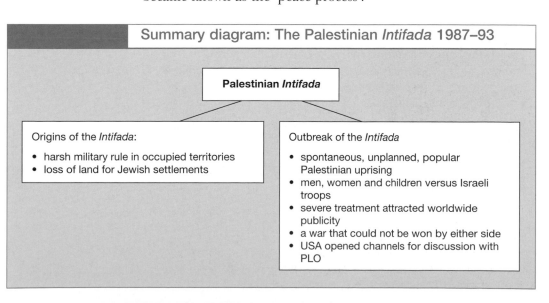

Summary diagram: The Palestinian *Intifada* 1987–93

Palestinian *Intifada*

Origins of the *Intifada*:
- harsh military rule in occupied territories
- loss of land for Jewish settlements

Outbreak of the *Intifada*
- spontaneous, unplanned, popular Palestinian uprising
- men, women and children versus Israeli troops
- severe treatment attracted worldwide publicity
- a war that could not be won by either side
- USA opened channels for discussion with PLO

Study Guide

In the style of OCR

To what extent do you agree that, without the use of terrorism, the Palestinians would have gained very little international support in the years to 1990?

Exam tips

The cross-references are intended to take you straight to the material that will help you to answer the question.

In this essay you need to analyse how much international support, if any, was achieved: (a) by terrorism or (b) by other means.

(a) By terrorism, you should explain the effects on international opinion of:

- Fatah's raids (although some would not class these as terrorism but as battling against the Israeli regime for an independent Palestine).
- The 'Battle of Karameh' in 1968 may not directly have won international support but certainly won more recruits for Fatah and significant international publicity (see page 80).
- More extreme methods such as hijackings and hostage-taking. Did these acts of terrorism win or lose support internationally? What was achieved by the Olympic killings? You might make use of the quotations on pages 82–3.

(b) By other means:

- The *Intifada*. Explain briefly what it was. What images of Palestinians did the world see? How, if at all, might this have gained international support? What were the effects on Israel and the USA (pages 88–9)?
- You might consider the effects on international opinion of the Israeli invasions of Lebanon and the massacres in the Palestinian refugee camps. This may not lead to any clear answer but you should, nonetheless, make an informed assessment as to whether any international support was gained (pages 84–6).

Think of any causal links you can make between the effects of terrorism in the 1970s and the *Intifada* in the 1980s. Why might the international response be more favourable in the 1980s?

   You might consider whether any significant level of international support was ever achieved by any means. That would then help you, finally, to make your concluding judgement about the importance of terrorism in winning international support.

6 The Challenges of Peace-making 1991–2008: Israelis and Palestinians

POINTS TO CONSIDER

This chapter will focus on the challenges of peace-making between the Israelis and the Palestinians. It will examine the successes of the 1990s as well as the obstacles that have hindered the subsequent development of the peace process.

These are considered under the following headings:

- The Israeli–Palestinian peace agreement 1993
- The problems of peace-making 1993–9
- The second *Intifada* and after 2000–8

Key dates

1974	Arafat's speech to the UN
1990	Iraqi invasion of Kuwait
1993 and 1995	Oslo Accords
1994	Israel–Jordan peace treaty
1995	Assassination of Rabin
2000	Camp David peace negotiations
	Beginning of the second *Intifada*
2002	Operation Defensive Shield
2003	'Road map' to peace
2004	Death of Yasser Arafat
	Mahmoud Abbas elected President of the Palestinian Authority
2006	Hamas victory in Palestinian elections
	Israeli invasion of Lebanon

1 | The Israeli–Palestinian Peace Agreement 1993

This chapter will concentrate on peace-making between Israelis and Palestinians in the 1990s and early twenty-first century. First, however, we must look at an earlier example of peace-making. In 1974, at the height of hijacking and hostage-taking by PLO extremists, Yasser Arafat and other moderate PLO leaders hinted that they were ready to consider a 'mini-state' for the Palestinians – consisting of the West Bank and Gaza where the majority of the inhabitants were Palestinian. In other words, they were no longer determined to destroy the state of Israel.

Arafat's speech to the United Nations 1974

At the end of 1974, Yasser Arafat was invited to speak at the UN. He told his audience that the Palestinian problem was about a people without a home, a people who had been forced to flee from their homes and who were still, after 25 years, living in refugee camps. Many of his listeners at the UN were sympathetic. Some world leaders were beginning to admit that the Palestinians deserved a homeland. They also realised that if the Palestinians were granted their wish, then permanent peace in the Middle East was possible.

Arafat gave his speech with a holster attached to his hip although he left the gun outside the hall. He ended the speech with the words:

> Today I have come bearing an olive branch [a symbol of peace] and a freedom fighter's gun. Do not let the olive branch fall from my hand.

Although he received a sympathetic hearing at the UN, there was no breakthrough to peace. The Israelis were furious with the UN for inviting Arafat to speak. They said the PLO was a 'murder organisation'. They refused to discuss the idea of a separate Palestinian state, however small it might be. They feared that the Palestinians aimed to take back all of Israel and would not be content with a small state next door to Israel. The PLO was itself divided. Some extremists still insisted that Israel should be completely destroyed and taken over by Palestinians. They rejected the idea of a Palestinian 'mini-state' and did not want any Arab state to recognise Israel.

Apart from the treaty between Egypt and Israel in 1979 (see page 58), there was little sign of peace breaking out in the Middle East until the 1990s.

The USA pushes for peace

At the height of the *Intifada*, in December 1988, the USA opened secret talks with PLO officials. The Americans persuaded Yasser Arafat to do something he had never done before publicly: he rejected terrorism. He also spoke out in favour of a two-state solution to the Israeli–Palestinian conflict: an independent Palestinian state *alongside* Israel. In other words, he recognised the state of Israel. Now, at last, the USA was willing to negotiate openly with the PLO and to urge the Israelis to open peace talks with the Palestinians.

At first, the Israeli government was in no mood for compromise. They viewed Arafat's announcement as a 'propaganda exercise' and said that the PLO was still just a terrorist organisation. The Israeli Prime Minister said 'No' to withdrawal from the occupied territories, 'No' to recognition of the PLO, 'No' to a Palestinian state.

Key question
What did Arafat achieve by speaking at the UN?

Key date
Arafat's speech to the UN: 1974

Key question
What impact did US diplomacy have on the PLO?

Key question
Why did the USA put more pressure on Israel to make peace with the PLO in the early 1990s?

Key date

Iraqi invasion of Kuwait: 1990

The Iraqi invasion of Kuwait 1990

The Americans were still determined to bring Israelis and Palestinians face to face at the negotiating table but, before any peace talks could be started, another conflict in the Middle East grabbed the headlines. In August 1990, Iraqi troops invaded Kuwait, a neighbouring Arab state, claiming that Kuwait belonged to them (see the map on page 112). Most of the Arab world, as well as other countries, condemned the Iraqi attack. The USA rushed troops to the Middle East. The UN called for Iraq to withdraw and the Americans led a huge multinational force which, by the end of February 1991, had driven the Iraqis out of Kuwait. This was known as the Gulf War, because Kuwait is on the Persian Gulf. It is explained more fully in Chapter 8.

Palestinians and other Arabs were quick to point out what they saw as the USA's double standards. They said that the Americans had acted swiftly to enforce the UN demand for Iraq to withdraw from Kuwait, yet they had not managed, even after 20 years, to persuade Israel to withdraw its troops from the occupied territories of Gaza and the West Bank. The UN had demanded this as far back as 1967 in the famous Resolution 242 (see page 53). The US government was stung by this criticism. It wanted to keep the support of Arab states such as Egypt, Saudi Arabia, even Syria, who had joined the USA in the fight against Iraq. Also, America's allies in the West depended on imports of oil from Arab states. So the US government was at last willing to put more pressure on Israel. It was also in a better position to do so now.

The end of the Cold War

The reason for this change was that the Cold War (between the USA and the Soviet Union) had now ended. The communist government in Russia was, by this time, collapsing. It could no longer support the Arab states so strongly. In fact, Russia was now desperately seeking US financial aid. Therefore, the US government could expect the co-operation not only of the Russians but also of Arab leaders who would no longer be able to rely on Russia for arms and money. All of this meant that the USA did not have to support Israel *in order to* contain a Russian threat in the Middle East any longer. The US government could therefore push the Israelis into making peace. In September 1991, the US President threatened to withhold $10 billion of loans to Israel. This threat had the desired effect.

The Madrid conference 1991

In October 1991, the US government persuaded the Israelis to hold face-to-face talks with Palestinian leaders. By now, an increasing number of both Israelis and Palestinians were coming to the conclusion that they had more to gain from making peace than making war. At the talks held in Madrid in Spain, the Palestinians spoke of the need for compromise but the Israeli leader, Yitzhak Shamir, was still intransigent and little progress was made in the talks. Meanwhile, the extremists on both sides attempted to disrupt the discussions by acts of violence. The USA, however, still kept up the pressure on Israel: in particular, the Americans called on the Israelis to stop building more settlements in the occupied territories or face the risk of losing their financial aid. When elections were held in Israel in 1992, a new, more moderate government was voted into power. This new government promised to work for peace with the Palestinians.

The Oslo Accord 1993

In 1993, discussions were started up again. This time they were held in secret, in Oslo, in neutral Norway, away from the glare of worldwide publicity. Fourteen sessions of talks were held over eight months. Finally, in September, the PLO leader, Yasser Arafat, and the head of the new Israeli government, Yitzhak Rabin, exchanged letters. Arafat, in his letter, rejected the use of terrorism, called for an end to the *Intifada* and recognised 'the right of Israel to exist in peace and security'. He had never made such clear statements before. Rabin, in his letter, recognised 'the PLO as the representative of the Palestinian people'. In the past, the Israeli government had refused to acknowledge the PLO and had regarded it as just a terrorist organisation.

On 13 September 1993, the two leaders signed an agreement, which became known as the **Oslo Accord**. This paved the way for a step-by-step approach towards self-government for the Palestinians. Then, in front of all the world's cameras at the White House in Washington, Arafat and Rabin shook hands. At last, a major breakthrough had been made in resolving the Palestinian problem. The *Daily Mail* wrote:

> Handshake for history. This was the moment no one had dared hope for, organised for a worldwide TV audience by President Clinton on the South Lawn of the White House. At Clinton's right hand was Israeli Prime Minister Yitzhak Rabin, a former general in the Six-Day War when Israel grabbed the occupied territories,

Key question
What was achieved by the 1993 peace agreement?

Key date
Oslo Accords: 1993 and 1995

Key term
Oslo Accord
The name given to the agreement resulting from peace negotiations held in Oslo.

Rabin (left) and Arafat (right) shake hands while US President Clinton looks on.

including Gaza and the West Bank, from the Arabs. To his left was Yasser Arafat, mastermind of a long terrorist war against Israel. Once bitter enemies, they were risking their political lives on an agreement giving Palestinians self-rule in the Gaza Strip and part of the West Bank in return for official recognition of the Jewish state.

What was agreed?
The Israeli and Palestinian leaders agreed that:

- Israeli troops would be withdrawn from Gaza and the city of Jericho (see the map on page 11) on the West Bank. After that, they would be withdrawn from other parts, but not all, of the West Bank. For instance, Israeli troops would *not* be withdrawn from their military bases, from Jewish settlements or from Jerusalem.
- Elections would be held for a **Palestinian Authority** (PA) to run the West Bank and Gaza for five years.
- During these five years a final settlement would be discussed.

The Oslo Accord was not really a peace treaty. It established a timetable for Palestinian self-government but it postponed any final settlement. The most difficult questions were to be settled over the next five years. (These are explained on page 96.) Nevertheless, it was a historic breakthrough because, after 46 years, the two sides had accepted the principle of partition which the UN had first proposed in 1947. Within a year, Israeli troops were withdrawn from Gaza and Jericho, as agreed. In July 1994, Yasser Arafat received a hero's welcome when he arrived in Gaza. It was the first time he had set foot on Palestinian soil for 27 years.

Oslo II Accord 1995
In 1995 a second Israeli–Palestinian agreement was signed. It became known as the Oslo II Accord. It was agreed that:

- elections to the Palestinian Authority would finally be held
- Israeli forces would withdraw from major Palestinian towns
- Palestinian prisoners would be released from Israeli jails.

When elections were held for the PA, the PLO won the majority of seats and Arafat was later elected President of the Palestinian Authority.

Israel–Jordan peace treaty 1994
In the wake of the Israeli–Palestinian agreement of 1993, Jordan signed a peace treaty with Israel in which the two sides settled their dispute over their borders. More importantly, Jordan became the second Arab state (after Egypt in 1978) to recognise the state of Israel and to open up trade and other links. Relations between Israel and Syria, however, remained very bitter and no agreement was reached on the return of the Golan Heights (see page 52) to Syria.

Key term

Palestinian Authority
A Palestinian 'government', with limited authority, in the West Bank and Gaza.

Key date

Israel–Jordan peace treaty: 1994

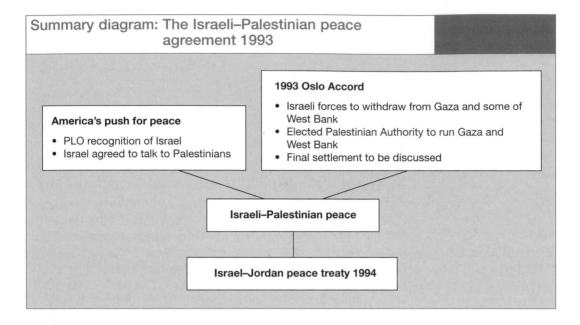

Summary diagram: The Israeli–Palestinian peace agreement 1993

America's push for peace

- PLO recognition of Israel
- Israel agreed to talk to Palestinians

1993 Oslo Accord

- Israeli forces to withdraw from Gaza and some of West Bank
- Elected Palestinian Authority to run Gaza and West Bank
- Final settlement to be discussed

Israeli–Palestinian peace

Israel–Jordan peace treaty 1994

2 | The Problems of Peace-making 1993–9

The Oslo peace agreements were intended to build confidence and trust between the Israelis and the Palestinians. This they did. The most difficult questions were to be discussed, over the five years from 1993 to 1998, before a final settlement was reached. The main issues were:

- *The future of Jerusalem.* Both Israelis and Palestinians wanted it as their capital. The Israelis were determined to ensure that they continued to control all of the city and that it remained *their* capital. By the late 1990s, east Jerusalem, which was mostly Arab, was encircled by Israeli settlements containing 150,000 Israelis.
- *Jewish settlements in the occupied territories.* What would happen to the numerous Jewish settlements on the West Bank? Should they be given up? If not, should Israeli troops continue to guard those settlements and protect the Jewish inhabitants?
- *An independent Palestinian state.* Would most Palestinians agree to a state which was limited to the West Bank and Gaza or would many demand all of Palestine (meaning the end of Israel)? Even if a Palestinian state was limited to the West Bank and Gaza, Palestinians would surely want a completely independent state. Yet if Israeli troops stayed on the West Bank, then it would not be part of a completely independent Palestine, simply because Israeli (i.e. foreign) troops were stationed there. The Israelis, for their part, were worried about their security. They suspected that many Palestinians would not be satisfied with a mini-state and that Israel would constantly face the threat of destruction.
- *The Palestinian refugees' right to return.* Would the refugees in Lebanon, Syria, Jordan and other Arab countries be allowed to

Key question
What were the issues to be resolved before a final settlement could be agreed?

return to the homes they had left during the fighting in 1948–9? Most Israelis believed that the Palestinians should not be allowed to return. The Israelis were not willing to turn their people out of the houses they had lived in, and off the land they had farmed, for many years. Besides, Israel would be swamped if all the Palestinian refugees returned and the Palestinians might then form the majority of the population of Israel! Yet, as an Arab information service in Britain wrote: 'Keeping millions of Palestinians without a homeland will amount to leaving an unexploded bomb under any peace agreement signed.'

Israeli and Palestinian views of the peace process

Key question
In what ways did Israeli and Palestinian views of the peace process differ?

The 1993 and 1995 Oslo Accords were greeted right across the world as a breakthrough. There was widespread confidence that the 'peace process' would lead to a final settlement of the Palestinian problem, the heart of the Middle East conflict. Yet, despite the handshake on the White House lawn and the subsequent agreements, there was still deep distrust. Above all, there were very different views of what the peace agreements meant. For the Israelis, the agreements meant that they would withdraw their troops from Gaza and some parts of the West Bank but still keep overall control. They still saw their troops having the main responsibility for security, both inside the West Bank and on its borders. After all, there were 200,000 Israeli settlers to protect. Also, the roads leading to the settlements and their water supplies had to be protected. All of this would require many troops.

By contrast, most of the Palestinians saw the peace agreement as the first step towards the establishment of an independent, Palestinian state. They saw the PA as the basis of a government which would lay the foundations for that new Palestinian state. The PA, however, was seen by most Israelis as a very limited form of self-government. For example, it might run schools and hospitals and set up a Palestinian police force to keep law and order among the Palestinian people. But the Israelis still saw themselves as remaining in overall control of security in Gaza and on the West Bank.

The peace process slows down

Key question
Why did the peace process slow down?

Over the next few years the pace of change was too slow for most Palestinians. The withdrawal of Israeli troops from Palestinian towns was very gradual and, worst of all from a Palestinian perspective, the Israelis kept on building Jewish settlements in the occupied territories. This involved the seizure of Palestinian land and often the demolition of their homes. It also meant the building of roads (which cut through Palestinian areas) for Jewish-only use and it meant more wells sunk to provide water for Jewish-only settlements.

The building of more Jewish settlements had not been banned in the Oslo agreements but, in the eyes of the Palestinians, it went against the spirit of the 'peace process'. It led to the takeover of more of their land. In their frustration and anger, many Palestinians switched their support from the PLO to more **militant** Palestinian groups. Among these groups was **Hamas**, whose initials in Arabic stood for the Islamic Resistance Movement.

Suicide bombings and assassination 1995–7

Hamas had opposed the 'peace process' because they believed that the Palestinians gained little. For a start, there was no Israeli recognition of Palestine's right to an independent Palestinian state, let alone the promise of such a state. Besides which, it was the declared aim of Hamas to destroy the state of Israel. Support for Hamas increased dramatically after a Jewish settler, Baruch Goldstein, went on the rampage and killed 29 Palestinians at a mosque in Hebron, on the West Bank, in 1994. Organisations like Hamas blamed the Israeli government for not disarming the settlers and for allowing this to happen. Israeli settlers had the army and police to protect them as well as being heavily armed themselves. Most Palestinians felt very vulnerable. Over the next few years, Hamas embarked on a campaign of suicide bombings, both in Israel itself and in the occupied territories. In July 1997, the *Guardian* newspaper carried a report of one such suicide bombing in Jerusalem:

> ### Horror in the Market Place
> *Israel Stunned as 15 Die in Suicide Bombing, Shattering Peace Hopes*
>
> The bombers dressed in black. They wore suits and ties and carried briefcases. They parked their car a few hundred yards from Jerusalem's market and walked into the dense mix of fruit, vegetables and heaving crowds. The two men were almost certainly in sight of one another when they pulled the cords on their twin bombs.
>
> By late last night, the toll was 15 dead and more than 150 wounded. All Palestinians working in Israel were ordered back to the West Bank and Gaza, which have been sealed off.
>
> Yasser Arafat, the Palestinian leader, declared a state of emergency yesterday in the territories controlled by his Palestinian Authority and began arresting Islamic militants. Leaflets circulating in Palestinian areas claimed the attack had been carried out by the main Palestinian extremist group, Hamas.
>
> 'I condemn completely this terrorist act because it is against the peace process, against the Palestinians and against the Israelis', said Arafat.

Bombings like this made the Israeli government take a harder line. They blamed Arafat and the PA for not controlling the militants; Israeli troops moved back into areas in Gaza and the West Bank which they had recently left. **Curfews** were imposed in

Key question
What effects did suicide bombings have?

Militant
A person who supports the use of force.

Hamas
Founded in Gaza in 1988 by Sheikh Ahmed Yassin, a religious teacher. The movement opposed the Oslo Accords and refused to recognise the state of Israel.

Curfew
A time or signal after which it was compulsory for people to remain indoors.

Key terms

A Palestinian woman argues with an Israeli soldier while being held at gunpoint in the West Bank town of Hebron. After clashes between Palestinians and Israeli security forces, the army imposed a curfew on the town in December 1996.

the towns, cities and refugee camps and the Israelis closed the border crossings between Israel and the occupied territories. They did this so as to seal their borders and prevent suicide bombers slipping through. But it also meant that Palestinians could not cross into Israel where many of them worked by day. This increased unemployment and hardship amongst the Palestinians. It also hurt the Israeli economy because many Israeli farms and factories depended on a plentiful supply of cheap Palestinian labour.

Despite these setbacks, talks between the Israeli government and the PA were still held, often in neutral, foreign countries. Agreements were made to withdraw Israeli troops from more Palestinian towns and cities on the West Bank and, in return, Arafat agreed to arrest Hamas militants. But, time and time again, it was the extremists on both sides who dominated the headlines. And it was not always Jew versus Arab or Arab versus Jew.

Key question
Why was Rabin assassinated?

Key date
Assassination of Rabin: 1995

The assassination of Rabin 1995

In November 1995, 150,000 Israelis gathered in Tel Aviv for a peace rally. The main speaker was the Prime Minister, Yitzak Rabin, who had signed the peace deal in 1993. After the rally, a young Israeli, Yigal Amir, stepped up and shot Rabin, who died on the way to hospital. The assassin was a member of an Israeli group that opposed any peace with the Palestinians. This group believed that the West Bank (which they called Judea and Samaria, as in the Bible) was part of the Land of Israel, the land which God had promised to the Jews. In their view, Rabin had been prepared to give away parts of the sacred Land of Israel and was thus a traitor and an enemy of the Jewish people. At his trial, Amir said: 'When I shot Rabin, I felt I was shooting a terrorist.' He was sentenced to life imprisonment.

The majority of Israelis supported the 'peace process'. They believed that it was worth exchanging land for security and accepted that, one day, there would have to be a Palestinian state based on the West Bank and Gaza. But, after a series of suicide bombings on crowded buses in Israeli towns, the hardliners in Israel gained more support. In May 1996, six months after the death of Rabin, a new government was elected in Israel. This government opposed the Oslo peace process and blocked any further negotiations with Arafat and the PA.

Building new Jewish settlements

In February 1997 the new Israeli government gave the go-ahead for the building of 6500 new homes on Arab land in east Jerusalem. This would complete a chain of Jewish settlements round the eastern side of Jerusalem and effectively cut off the Arab inhabitants of east Jerusalem from the rest of the West Bank (see the map on page 104). This further dashed Palestinian hopes of making east Jerusalem the capital of an independent state of Palestine.

As the bulldozers went into action to clear the ground for building to start, the new Israeli Prime Minister, Binyamin Netanyahu, announced; 'The battle for Jerusalem has begun.' For most Palestinians, the Israeli Prime Minister was not a peace-maker but the leader of a brutal occupying power.

Key question
What was the effect of new settlement building?

An Israeli bulldozer prepares to flatten an Arab house on the West Bank, February 1997, to make way for a larger Jewish settlement. What impact did settlement building have on the peace process?

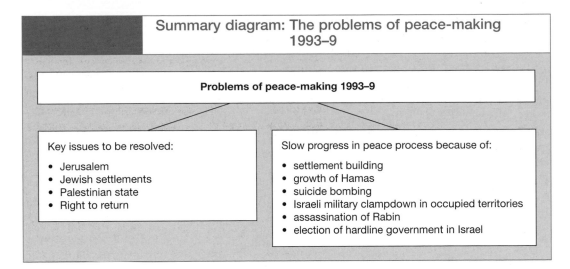

Summary diagram: The problems of peace-making 1993–9

Problems of peace-making 1993–9

Key issues to be resolved:

- Jerusalem
- Jewish settlements
- Palestinian state
- Right to return

Slow progress in peace process because of:

- settlement building
- growth of Hamas
- suicide bombing
- Israeli military clampdown in occupied territories
- assassination of Rabin
- election of hardline government in Israel

3 | The Second *Intifada* and After 2000–8

Clinton's final bid for peace, Camp David 2000

Key question
What was the outcome of the talks at Camp David?

In 1999 there was yet another change of government in Israel and, this time, the Israelis elected a more moderate government led by Ehud Barak. The US President, Bill Clinton, tried to revive the peace process. In July 2000, he invited the Israeli and PLO leaders to Camp David. For several days the two sides were locked in discussion, with the Americans trying to steer the negotiations towards a peaceful outcome. Barak offered the Palestinians a deal that would have given them Gaza and most of the West Bank. And he went further than any previous Israeli Prime Minister by agreeing to partition the city of Jerusalem. But the obstacles to peace proved too great. In particular, the issues of who controlled the holy sites of Jerusalem and of the right of Palestinian refugees to return to Israel could not be resolved. The talks ended with no significant progress achieved. Many in the West blamed Arafat, accusing him of rejecting a generous deal. Others defended him: how could the PLO accept a peace deal that did not grant them complete control of east Jerusalem, which was mainly Arab, as their capital?

Key dates
Camp David peace negotiations: 2000

Beginning of the second *Intifada*: 2000

The second *Intifada* 2000

Key question
What were the origins of the second *Intifada*?

On 28 September 2000 the Israeli politician, Ariel Sharon, made a tour of what Jews call Temple Mount in Jerusalem. To Muslims, this area is known as the Dome of the Rock (see the photograph on page 12 showing the golden dome of the al-Aqsa mosque) and is their third holiest site after Mecca and Medina. Sharon obviously expected to cause trouble as he was accompanied by over 1000 police! He certainly got it. The visit was seen as highly provocative by Palestinians. Many saw it as a threat to impose Israeli control over the holy sites. Whatever the intentions, demonstrations followed and Israeli troops shot seven Palestinians dead and wounded over 200. This marked the start of a second *Intifada*; within a month 127 Palestinians had been killed.

The underlying cause of this second *Intifada* was the frustration and anger of the Palestinians in the occupied territories of the West Bank and in Gaza. Seven years after the Oslo peace agreement, little progress had been made in the peace process, especially over the key issues – the borders of a future Palestinian state, the status of Jerusalem, Jewish settlements in the occupied territories and the right of Palestinian refugees to return to Israel. For many, both in Israel and on the West Bank and in Gaza, things had worsened: Palestinian suicide bombings, Israeli reprisals and the building of more Jewish settlements continued. Between 1993 and 2000, there was a 77 per cent increase in the number of Jewish settlers in the occupied territories. The Palestinians, in particular, felt that they were hemmed in:

- In Gaza, which is smaller than the Isle of Wight, there were a million Palestinians, half of them in refugee camps and dependent on UN hand-outs, living in a thin strip of land between the sea and the Israeli border. There were only 6500 Jewish settlers but they and the troops protecting them controlled a third of the land and most of the water supplies.
- On the West Bank and around Jerusalem there were nearly 400,000 Jewish settlers and tens of thousands of troops. There were over two million Palestinians but the Israelis controlled over 70 per cent of the land and had complete control of the water and electricity supplies. The Israelis controlled the main roads and they restricted the movements of the Palestinians with checkpoints, road blocks and night-time curfews.

The Israelis seemed to be consolidating their hold on the land. A more permanent peace and an independent Palestinian state seemed more distant than ever.

The attack on the World Trade Center in New York 2001
On 11 September 2001, four US passenger planes were hijacked and two of them were flown into the twin towers of the World Trade Center building in New York, leading to the deaths of nearly 3000 people. To Americans, these are known as the events of '9/11' after the date on which they occurred. (They are explained more fully on page 148.) From now onwards, Israel frequently portrayed itself as a nation engaged in the 'war on terror', like its US ally. Ariel Sharon is reported to have said: 'Everyone has his own Bin Laden and Arafat is ours.' The Americans were not impressed. Arafat was the first Arab leader to condemn '9/11'. He stressed that the Palestinians' struggle was mainly a political and national struggle whereas Bin Laden's war against the West was a religious one. He also emphasised that Palestinians only used violence in self-defence, in their resistance to Israeli occupation.

Key question
How was Operation
Defensive Shield
carried out?

Key date

Operation Defensive
Shield: 2002

Operation Defensive Shield, March 2002

In February 2001 Ariel Sharon was elected Prime Minister of
Israel. He promised to maintain Israeli sovereignty over
Jerusalem and to increase the number of settlements on the West
Bank. Meanwhile, the death toll in the Middle East mounted.
Hamas and other militant Palestinian groups carried out
bombings both inside Israel and also against Israeli troops and
settlers in the occupied territories. In March 2002, after 29
Israelis were killed in a Hamas suicide bombing, Sharon launched
'Operation Defensive Shield'.

In order to root out the 'terrorists', Israeli troops and tanks
carried out raids inside Palestinian towns and refugee camps on
the West Bank and Gaza. They attacked and surrounded Arafat's
headquarters in the West Bank town of Ramallah. They also
embarked on a policy of targeted assassinations, often using
helicopter gunships in order to kill Palestinian militants in their
homes or offices. They even used fighter planes to bomb their
targets; not surprisingly, women and children, often family
members, were also killed. Schools and hospitals were sometimes
hit. These buildings may have contained Hamas members but
then organisations like Hamas also ran schools and hospitals as
well as carrying out military activities. Life in the occupied
territories became worse and worse. Fresh water and food became
more scarce and very few people had paid work.

Key question
What was the
purpose of the
security barrier?

Israel's security barrier

By May 2003, over 2000 Palestinians and 760 Israelis had been
killed since the *Intifada* started in 2000. This was a far higher
number than in the first *Intifada*. In this second *Intifada*, many

Israel's security barrier.

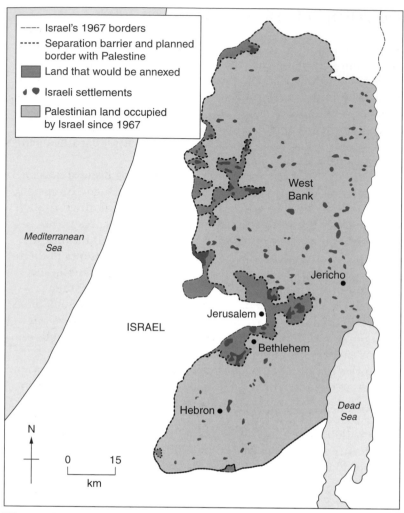

Key:
- ---- Israel's 1967 borders
- ..... Separation barrier and planned border with Palestine
- Land that would be annexed
- ◀ ● Israeli settlements
- Palestinian land occupied by Israel since 1967

Mediterranean Sea

West Bank

Jericho

Jerusalem ●

ISRAEL

Bethlehem ●

Hebron ●

Dead Sea

N

0   15

km

Why were so many settlements built around Jerusalem?

Palestinians used rifles rather than stones and the Israelis used rockets, tanks and helicopters. As the violence continued, Israel started to build a barrier around the West Bank. In some places, it was an eight-metre high concrete wall, in other places it was just a fence. It was reinforced by troops, barbed wire and surveillance cameras. The wall was not built along the **'green line'** that marked the pre-1967 boundary between Israel and the occupied territories, but was further into the West Bank (see the map above).

Israelis said the wall was temporary and purely defensive, to keep out the bombers, but its opponents said it took more land from the Palestinians. They pointed out that many West Bank Jewish settlements were on the Israeli side and that some Palestinian villages found themselves on the 'wrong side'. In other words, the Israelis were creating 'facts on the ground' so that any future Palestinian state would not include all of the West Bank occupied by Israel in the 1967 war.

'Green line'
The border between Israel and the West Bank before the 1967 Six-Day War.

Key term

Key question
What did the 'road map' achieve?

Key dates

'Road map' to peace: 2003

Death of Yasser Arafat: 2004

Mahmoud Abbas elected President of the Palestinian Authority: 2004

'Road map' to peace 2003

In April 2003 US President George W. Bush published what he called a 'road map' for peace between Israel and the Palestinians. His country was about to invade Iraq in order to topple the government of Saddam Hussein (see page 136) and he was keen to show he was just as concerned about the Palestinian problem as he was about oil-rich Iraq. The road map outlined a timetable for moves towards a Palestinian state. The first phase was to depend on an end to Palestinian bombings, to Israeli raids on Palestinian towns and to settlement building.

At first, the 'road map' made little difference. The Palestinian bombings continued and so did Israel's targeted assassinations. In March 2004, an Israeli helicopter missile killed the spiritual leader of Hamas as he left a mosque near his home in Gaza. However, over the next two years, there were signs of a revival in the peace process. In April 2004, the Israeli government announced that it would evacuate all Jewish settlers and troops from Gaza. In November 2004, Yasser Arafat died and was succeeded by Mahmoud Abbas who became Chairman of the PLO and was elected President of the Palestinian Authority. In February 2005, Abbas persuaded Palestinian militants to call a halt, even if only temporary, to their bombing. Then the Israeli and Palestinian leaders met in Egypt and announced a mutual ceasefire. In the summer of 2005, Jewish settlers and troops were withdrawn from Gaza.

Nevertheless, the issue of Jewish settlements on the West Bank remained the greatest obstacle to peace. For the peace process to succeed, trust between the two sides was necessary. Although Palestinian violence undoubtedly contributed to the breakdown of trust, the fundamental reason was the Israeli policy of expanding settlements on the West Bank. This policy was carried on under both hardline and more moderate Israeli governments and it prevented the emergence of a viable Palestinian state without which there could be no end to the conflict.

A cartoon from *The Times*, March 2004. It follows the killing of Hamas leader, Sheikh Ahmed Yassin, a paralysed man who had to use a wheelchair. In the tank is Israeli Prime Minister, Ariel Sharon. What is the message of the cartoon?

Profile: Yasser Arafat 1929–2004

1929	– Born into a middle-class Palestinian family
1948	– Fought in the first Arab–Israeli War
1949	– Studied engineering in Egypt, becoming President of Palestinian Students Union
1959	– Founded Fatah while working as an engineer in Kuwait
1969	– Became Chairman of the PLO
1974	– Addressed the UN General Assembly
1988	– Publicly recognised the state of Israel for the first time
1993	– Signed Oslo peace agreement with the Israelis
1994	– Awarded Nobel Peace Prize for his role in peace-making
1996	– Elected President of the Palestinian Authority
2004	– Died

Arafat fled to Egypt, aged 20, when the state of Israel was created and became one of a small group of young Palestinians who were students together in Cairo and who later, when working in Kuwait, formed Fatah. They dedicated themselves to the 'armed struggle' to liberate Palestine: that single aim was all-important, more so than waiting for a united Arab response which some Palestinians thought should come first.

In the 1960s Arafat was involved actively in operations against Israel and, for security reasons, he slept in a different bed every night. He was widely respected as a freedom fighter although many Israelis described him as a terrorist. The 'Battle of Karameh' (see page 80) in Jordan in 1968 was a major turning point as it brought him international recognition and a huge increase in recruits to Fatah. By 1970, about 40,000 fighters had been trained in Jordan. After 1970, when the PLO was expelled from Jordan (see page 81), most of the Palestinian armed forces were based in Lebanon.

During the siege of Beirut in 1982, when the Israeli army surrounded the largely civilian population of Beirut and bombarded it daily, Arafat toured the city endlessly, visiting the PLO frontlines, bread queues, refugee camps and hospitals.

The success of the *Intifada* in 1987–8 gave Arafat and the PLO leadership the confidence to seize the initiative and take the bold step of renouncing terrorism, recognising the state of Israel and demanding that the Israelis leave the occupied territories and agree to a Palestinian state on the West Bank and in Gaza. This alienated many of those Palestinians in refugee camps who realised that their 'right to return' to their original homes in Israel was being ignored but pleased those living in the occupied territories who had suffered over 20 years of Israeli military control.

Five years later, Arafat signed a peace deal with the Israelis and, in 1994, he stepped on to Palestinian soil, in Gaza, for the first time in 27 years. When the peace process stalled at the turn of the century, Arafat faced new challenges from groups like Hamas who rejected any deals with Israel. When Israeli troops re-entered the West Bank in 2002 they effectively surrounded Arafat in his headquarters in Ramallah. He died in 2004.

Key question
What was the significance of the Hamas election victory in 2006?

Key dates

Hamas victory in Palestinian elections: 2006

Israeli invasion of Lebanon: 2006

Hamas victory in Palestinian elections 2006

In 2006 elections were held for the Palestinian parliament. All adult Palestinians on the West Bank and in Gaza were entitled to vote. Up until that time, most of the seats in the parliament had been held by members of Fatah, which was the main body inside the PLO. Increasingly, however, ordinary Palestinians saw Fatah and many of the PLO leaders as corrupt and ineffective. There was widespread frustration, anger and bitterness about the poverty and squalor in which so many Palestinians lived.

Hamas won the majority of seats in the elections. Mahmoud Abbas, a member of Fatah, remained as President of the Palestinian Authority. He also maintained his contacts with members of the Israeli government but the Hamas majority in the Palestinian parliament refused to recognise the state of Israel. As a result, Israel, the USA and most European governments refused to have any dealings with Hamas. The peace process stalled yet again.

War in Lebanon 2006

In 2000, the Israelis withdrew their last troops from southern Lebanon. They had originally occupied the area in order to protect their northern border but they faced increasing guerrilla attacks from Hizbollah, a militant Lebanese organisation whose main support came from Muslims in the south. (Hizbollah was backed by Syria and the Islamic government in Iran.)

In July 2006, Hizbollah fighters crossed the border into Israel, killed three Israeli soldiers and captured two others. They then demanded the release of hundreds of Hizbollah fighters and Palestinians who were held in Israeli jails. Israel refused to agree to a swap and launched air attacks on Hizbollah strongholds, in both south Lebanon and Beirut, the capital. Hizbollah hit back by launching hundreds of missiles, from the south of Lebanon, against towns in the north of Israel.

Israeli planes bombed Beirut airport and bridges leading to Syria which they believed to be the source of Hizbollah missiles. Within a month, the death toll in Lebanon reached a thousand, mostly civilians, with nearly a million made homeless. Nearly 100 Israelis were killed. In August 2006, a ceasefire was arranged at the UN and fighting stopped. A UN peacekeeping force was sent to the Israeli–Lebanese border. The Israelis had failed to destroy Hizbollah or to recover their captured soldiers. In the Arab world, Hizbollah's 'victory' was seen as proof that a small (Islamic) guerrilla force could defeat the most heavily armed state in the Middle East. The Israel–Lebanon border remains a likely flashpoint for future conflict.

Fighting in Gaza

Prospects for peace deteriorated yet further in 2007. Security forces under the control of President Abbas frequently clashed with supporters of Hamas in the West Bank and Gaza. Fighting broke out in Gaza between the armed forces of Hamas and those of Fatah. Hamas forces took control, destroying Fatah's headquarters and driving Fatah forces out of Gaza. Since then Hamas has dominated Gaza while the Fatah-dominated forces of Mahmoud Abbas have run the Palestinian-controlled parts of the West Bank.

Israeli forces sealed the border between Gaza and Israel and took complete control of movement, of both people and goods, in and out of Gaza. They also controlled movement in and out of Gaza by air and sea. The 1.4 million inhabitants of Gaza were virtually imprisoned. In 2008, there was a spate of rockets fired from Gaza into southern Israel. The Israelis retaliated, carrying out aerial bombing raids on Gaza as well as an invasion by land forces. They killed many Hamas militants as well as hundreds of civilians.

Prospects for Israeli–Palestinian peace

> **Key question**
> What will be required for a lasting peace between Palestinians and Israelis?

At the end of 2008 the heart of the conflict in the Middle East still remained Palestine and the problem of a people without a homeland. It is now harder than at any time since the 1993 agreements to envisage a viable Palestinian state. On the West Bank, Israeli settlements, with their roads and military bases, control 40 per cent of the territory. Peace-making is further complicated by the fact that the Palestinian leadership is deeply divided between Fatah and Hamas. Israel continues to talk to Mahmoud Abbas and the Fatah-dominated Palestinian Authority on the West Bank but refuses to negotiate with Hamas leaders in Gaza. Although Hamas has refused to recognise Israel (like Arafat and PLO leaders before the 1990s), its spokesmen have spoken of the possibility of a long-term truce in return for a Palestinian state based on 1967 borders.

The real test of peace-making will be the success which both Israeli and Palestinian leaders have in keeping the support of the majority of their people. On both sides there will always be extremists and those who oppose any compromise. On the Israeli side are those who believe that the West Bank must remain in Israeli hands because it is the 'promised land' that God gave to the Jews. On the Palestinian side are those who still believe that all of Palestine must be restored to the Palestinians, even if it means the destruction of Israel.

After 60 years of war, millions of Israelis and Palestinians want peace. The economies of both Israelis and Palestinians are devastated by violence. Israel knows that about 200,000 of its citizens are emigrating each year (mostly to the USA) and that, the longer the violence continues, the more this number will increase. Meanwhile, the Palestinian population grows. This may be one reason why the Israelis have built the wall, their security barrier; many Israelis are happy for the Palestinians to have a state of their own as long as it is enclosed. But a settlement dictated by one side will not bring lasting peace.

The main issues remain the same as ever:

- the borders of any Palestinian state
- the Jewish settlements on the West Bank
- the future of Jerusalem
- the Palestinian refugees' right to return.

Both sides have much to gain from discussion and negotiation but it will require great courage from their leaders. Syria will also have to be brought into the peace process. Unlike Egypt and Jordan, Syria has never made a peace treaty with Israel. Syria has still not regained the Golan Heights which Israel captured in 1967.

Above all, peace-making will require the wholehearted support of the US government. The USA is the only country that can put enough pressure on Israel to reach a negotiated settlement with the Palestinians and, at the same time, assure the Jewish state of its protection. The USA supplies Israel with over $3 billion of aid every year as well as the most advanced military equipment. Therefore it has huge influence in peace-making.

Only when peace between Israel and the Palestinians is secure will the threat from terrorism, in both the Middle East and the world as a whole, be reduced.

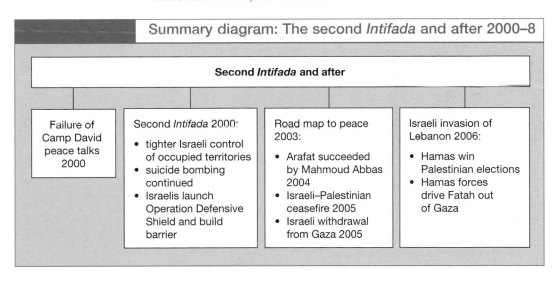

Summary diagram: The second *Intifada* and after 2000–8

Second *Intifada* and after

| Failure of Camp David peace talks 2000 | Second *Intifada* 2000:
 • tighter Israeli control of occupied territories
 • suicide bombing continued
 • Israelis launch Operation Defensive Shield and build barrier | Road map to peace 2003:
 • Arafat succeeded by Mahmoud Abbas 2004
 • Israeli–Palestinian ceasefire 2005
 • Israeli withdrawal from Gaza 2005 | Israeli invasion of Lebanon 2006:
 • Hamas win Palestinian elections
 • Hamas forces drive Fatah out of Gaza |

Study Guide

In the style of Edexcel and OCR

How far do you agree that Palestinian terrorism was the *main* reason for the failure to establish lasting peace between Israel and the Palestinians from 1973 to 2003?

Exam tips

The cross-references are intended to take you straight to the material that will help you to answer the question.

Re-read Chapters 5 and 6.

In this essay you have to analyse the effects of Palestinian terrorism, as well as other obstacles to lasting peace, before making a judgement on whether terrorism was the *main* factor. It is probably best to focus first on the obstacles to peace *before* the signing of the Oslo Accords in 1993 and *then* on the difficulties/issues that were specific to the period after 1993.

On the earlier period, covered in Chapter 5, you should assess the influence of:

- Palestinian opposition to the state of Israel and frequent resort to violence (although this will need to be qualified, e.g. Arafat at the UN in 1974) (page 92)
- cross-border raids on Israel by PLO and Israeli reprisals (including invasion of Lebanon)
- international terrorism in the 1970s, e.g. hijackings and murders at the Olympics.

Equally, you need to assess the degree of Israel's responsibility:

- Israel's occupation of all or most of Gaza and the West Bank and its unwillingness to recognise the PLO
- building of Jewish settlements in the occupied territories
- Israeli military rule in the occupied territories
- how far these factors contributed to the Palestinian *Intifada* from 1987, i.e. Israeli policy leading to Palestinian violence (pages 87–8).

On the period after 1993 (Chapter 6) you need to explain:

- conflicting Israeli and Palestinian views of the Oslo Accords (page 97)
- continued Israeli settlement building, especially on the West Bank
- suicide bombings by Palestinians
- the second *Intifada* and the Israeli response.

Throughout the essay you should try to identify the causal links between Israeli policy and Palestinian terrorism (and vice versa) as part of your assessment of whether Palestinian terrorism was the chief obstacle to peace. In conclusion, you need to weigh up the importance of Palestinian terrorism in the context of other obstacles to permanent peace and, finally, make your judgement about whether it was the *main* factor.

7 The Iran–Iraq War 1980–8

Key dates

1919	British granted a mandate over Iraq
1953	Overthrow of Mossadeq's government in Iran
1958	Iraqi army overthrew the monarchy
1968	Baathists seized power in Iraq
1979	Saddam Hussein became President of Iraq
	Iranian Revolution led by Ayatollah Khomeini
1980–8	Iran–Iraq War

1 | Iraq and the Rise of Saddam Hussein

Iraq lies in the ancient land of Mesopotamia, one of the world's oldest civilisations. The first cities were built here, the most famous of which was Baghdad. The Hanging Gardens of Babylon, built over 2000 years ago, became one of the Seven Wonders of the Ancient World. Many centuries later, in the seventh century AD, the land of Iraq was invaded by the Arabs and its people adopted both the language, Arabic, and the religion, Islam, of the invaders. Then, from the sixteenth century, Iraq was ruled by the Ottoman Turks.

Iraq in the First World War

Key question
Why was Iraq important to the British?

At the beginning of the twentieth century the British, as well as other European countries, were keen to gain a foothold in Iraq. The main reason was oil. Oil had been discovered in the south of Iran, near the Iraqi border, and was likely to be present in Iraq. At this time, Britain's navy, the largest in the world, was

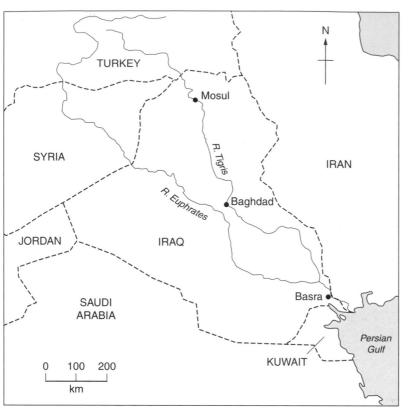

Iraq and its neighbours.

converting from coal to oil to fuel its ships, so oil was vital to Britain's defence needs.

When the First World War broke out in 1914, Turkey sided with Germany. Britain was keen to defeat Turkey and extend British influence, so British forces landed at Basra, in the south of Iraq (see the above map). This was the area where oil was later discovered. By 1917 the British had advanced to Baghdad and, a year later, they took Mosul. This meant that, in 1918, when the war ended, the British controlled the three provinces (Basra, Baghdad and Mosul) of what had been Turkish-ruled Iraq. The British commander announced: 'Our armies do not come into your cities and lands as conquerors or enemies, but as liberators.'

However, in 1916, Britain had agreed, with the French, to carve up Turkey's Arab lands when the war ended. This was in the Sykes–Picot Agreement (see page 8) under which Iraq was one of the countries assigned to Britain. At the end of the war the Treaty of Versailles recognised the British occupation of Iraq as a mandate according to which Iraq was to remain under British control 'until such time as it is able to stand alone'.

British granted mandate over Iraq: 1919

Key date

The British mandate in Iraq

This was a harsh blow to Iraqi nationalists, those who wanted (and, in some cases, had fought for) complete independence for Iraq. The British soon had a rebellion on their hands. They crushed it but they soon realised they could not run the country on their own. They needed collaborators. So they planned to set up an Iraqi state which would be independent but tied to Britain. In 1921, they invited Faisal, son of Sharif Hussein of Mecca to become King of Iraq and head of a new government. It was Faisal who had led the Arab Revolt against the Turks in the war (see page 8).

The borders of the new state of Iraq were not yet clear and the British had to stave off attacks from neighbouring Turkey and Iran. Nevertheless, the new monarchy got off to a good start and was to last for over 35 years. However, the country was far from independent: the British kept control of Iraq's foreign policy and kept two airbases (near Basra and Baghdad). Above all, they controlled the oil: they did this through the British-owned Iraqi Petroleum Company which owned, drilled and sold all of Iraq's oil.

The end of the Iraqi monarchy 1958

During the time of the monarchy, Iraq saw considerable economic development, education was improved and illiteracy reduced. But the country was dominated by a small number of big landowners while the vast majority of the population were landless peasants. There was widespread discontent. Above all, there was much resentment of foreign (i.e. British) control.

In 1952 the Iraqi government persuaded the Iraqi Petroleum Company to agree that the profits from oil would be shared equally between the Iraqi government and the British-dominated company. But the company still controlled production and prices. Added resentment was caused by Britain's role in establishing the state of Israel on Arab land. Furthermore, many Iraqis disliked the fact that their country was a member of the Western-dominated Baghdad Pact (see page 67). This had been set up by Britain, with Turkey, Iraq, Iran and Pakistan as members, in order to prevent the expansion of Soviet influence in the Middle East. Most Iraqis, however, wanted to be neutral.

In 1958 the Iraqi army carried out a coup which overthrew the monarchy and established a republic. The new government took Iraq out of the Baghdad Pact and persuaded Britain, which wanted to keep on good terms with the new government, to withdraw its troops. The Iraqi government also secured more control over oil production.

In the 1960s the call for Arab unity won much support in Iraq. The champion of Arab unity was President Nasser of Egypt. There was considerable support, in Iraq, for the United Arab Republic which had been formed between Egypt and Syria in 1958 (see page 70) but the military government resisted pressure to join. Nevertheless, the **Baath** Party became increasingly popular in Iraq. The Baathists called for unity among the Arabs throughout the Middle East. However, in Iraq, they were mainly supported because they demanded a strong stand in the face of foreign interference in the affairs of Iraq.

Key question
Why did the monarchy end in 1958?

Key date
Iraqi army overthrew the monarchy: 1958

Key term
Baath
Means 'Renaissance' or rebirth of Arab power. The Baath Party had originally been established in Syria in the 1950s but its influence extended to several Arab countries.

The Baathists seize power 1968

The Baathists, supported by some army officers, seized power in 1968. Most of them were Sunni Muslims. The Sunnis had been the dominant group in Iraq ever since the state of Iraq was set up in 1921, although the Shiite Muslims formed the majority of the population. Many Shiites were now brought into the new government in a show of unity. More money was spent on defence and the army, in particular. In 1972, the Baathist government nationalised, and took complete control of, the Iraqi oil industry, despite the opposition of the British. This was a daring and popular move.

Key question
How did the Baathists extend their power?

Baathists seized power: 1968

Key date

Sunni and Shiite

There was a major disagreement over who should succeed Muhammad as the Caliph, or leader (in Arabic, it literally means deputy or successor) of the Muslim world. Ali, the cousin and son-in-law of Muhammad, believed he should be leader and was recognised as Caliph in Iraq and Persia (modern Iran). But the Syrian Muslim rulers chose another successor. This led to a great division and warfare among Muslims with the creation of two groups: the Shia, or Shiite, Muslims who followed Ali, and the Sunni Muslims. Most of the Arabs became Sunni Muslims while the Arabs of southern Iraq and the (non-Arab) Persians became Shiite Muslims.

Then, in 1973, the Iraqis joined other Arab oil-producing states in reducing oil production and sales to Western countries. This was done to punish the West, who depended on oil from the Middle East, for their support of Israel in the Yom Kippur War (see page 56). However, it also had the effect of driving up oil prices by 400 per cent. Iraq's income from oil was to rise from $575 million in 1972 to $26,500 million in 1980.

As the country became richer, the Baathists brought about undoubted improvements: electricity was extended to the countryside; and roads, bridges, hospitals, schools and dams were built. The Iraqis became a more educated population and health care improved. An urban middle class of lawyers, businessmen and government officials emerged. The Baathists also became much more powerful, extending their control over Iraqi government and society. Trade unions, schools and even sports clubs came under state control and membership of the Baath Party determined public appointments. The main aim of education was to immunise the young against foreign culture and promote Arab unity and 'love of order'. The ideal student was one who could 'stand in the sun holding his weapon day and night without flinching'. So said the up-and-coming strong man in the government, Saddam Hussein.

Saddam Hussein and rule by terror

In the 1970s Saddam Hussein was the government minister responsible for extending government control over the army and the secret police. High military spending kept the armed forces happy but they were also kept under control by regular indoctrination, by rotating the officers (so that none stayed in one position, and could build up opposition, for long) and by the imprisonment and execution of those suspected of disloyalty.

Repression was extended throughout Iraqi society. There were increasing reports of torture and rape of those held in prison. The **Kurds**, in the north of Iraq, lost much of their self-government and many of their leaders were executed or driven into exile. The government, dominated by Sunnis, depended increasingly on the support of the rural, Sunni areas to the north of Baghdad even though the majority of the population were Shiites in the south and centre of Iraq. These divisions, between Sunnis, Shiites and Kurds, were to become more pronounced in the years to come.

Saddam Hussein becomes President of Iraq 1979

In 1979, Saddam Hussein became President of Iraq. His presidency started with the televised trial of a number of men, 21 of whom were later executed. This was not a completely new development: for some years, members of the Baath Party, as well as opponents of the government, had been tried and executed. But Saddam was certainly showing how he meant to continue: he was an admirer of Stalin's use of terror. The death penalty became the punishment for concealing previous membership of a different political party as well as for leaving the Baath Party to join another party. There were to be many attempts to overthrow Saddam, and two major defeats in war, but he was to hold on to power for nearly 25 years.

Since the end of the monarchy in 1958, some Kurds and many Shiites had done well and become better off in Iraq as long as they proved loyal. But, under Saddam, there were mass expulsions, first of Kurds, then of Shiites. In 1980–1, 200,000 Shiites were deported to Iran as their 'loyalty was not proven'. Many of them were successful businessmen whose businesses were then handed over to the government's supporters.

Key term

Kurds
The Kurds are Muslims but not Arab. They form about 20 per cent of the Iraqi population and are concentrated in the north of the country.

Key question
How did Saddam Hussein's government rule Iraq?

Key date

Saddam Hussein became President of Iraq: 1979

Saddam Hussein: President of Iraq 1979–2003.

Saddam increasingly assumed the role of leader of the Arab world. His government became much more anti-Israeli in its propaganda: it opposed the Egypt–Israel peace treaty of 1979, accusing Egypt of betraying the Arab cause. Meanwhile Saddam himself was glorified. Statues of him were erected everywhere, his portraits hung in all public buildings and his birthday was made a national holiday. When a referendum was held on his presidency (undoubtedly rigged), 99 per cent voted in support. He was portrayed as a national hero, dedicated to his people.

Summary diagram: Iraq and the rise of Saddam Hussein

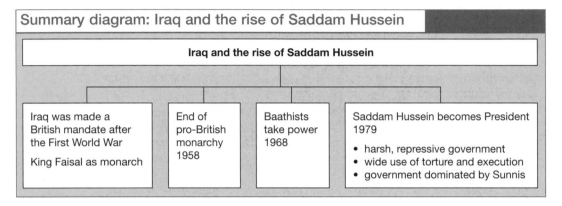

Iraq and the rise of Saddam Hussein

Iraq was made a British mandate after the First World War King Faisal as monarch	End of pro-British monarchy 1958	Baathists take power 1968	Saddam Hussein becomes President 1979 • harsh, repressive government • wide use of torture and execution • government dominated by Sunnis

2 | The Iranian Revolution 1979

Iran used to be called Persia and, like Iraq, was home to one of the great civilisations of the world. Iran is three times as big as Iraq, in both land area and population. It has long borders with Iraq to its west and Russia to the north (see the map below). It is a Muslim country but it is different to its Arab neighbours in two major ways. First, its people are mostly non-Arab and do not speak Arabic. Secondly, it is mostly made up of Shia, not Sunni, Muslims.

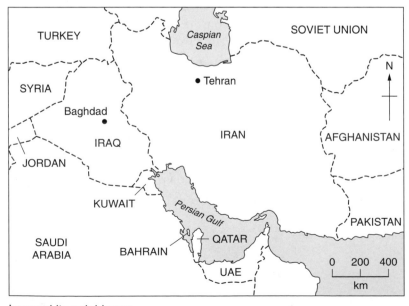

Iran and its neighbours.

Key question
Why was Iran so important to the British?

Key term

Shah
The title of the King or Emperor of Iran. It is similar to Tsar, the name of the Russian monarch, or Kaiser, the German emperor.

Iran under the Shah

At the start of the twentieth century, Iran was ruled by a monarch, known as the **Shah**. Iran was independent but the oilfields in the south were controlled by a British company that paid the Shah's government for the right to operate the oilfields. So, as in Iraq, the British controlled the oilfields, mainly in order to fuel the navy, and most of the profits went to the British company. It is important to remember that Britain was the world's greatest imperial power in the early twentieth century: it governed much of what is today India, Pakistan and Bangladesh, as well as Malaysia, Burma, Singapore and Hong Kong further east.

After the Second World War, an increasing number of Iranians demanded that their government take control of the oilfields. They insisted that their government should get at least half of the oil profits rather than most of them going to the British-owned Anglo-Iranian Oil Company (which later became the British Petroleum Company, or BP). The leading Iranian nationalist was Mohammed Mossadeq, a member of the Iranian parliament. He argued that: 'The oil resources of Iran, like its soil, its rivers and mountains, are the property of the people of Iran.'

Mossadeq gained huge popular support and, in 1951, the Shah was forced to appoint him Prime Minister. The Iranian parliament then passed a law to nationalise the oil industry so that Iranians, not the British, were in charge. This defiant move thrilled the Iranians. Many in the Arab world also applauded and Mossadeq became a hero to millions, both in and beyond Iran.

In retaliation the British company withdrew its workforce and refused to allow any of its technicians work with the new Iranian National Oil Company. The British also persuaded other Western oil companies not to buy Iran's oil and the British navy imposed a blockade on Iran's ports.

Key question
What was the significance of the 1953 coup?

Key date

Overthrow of Mossadeq's government in Iran: 1953

The overthrow of Mossadeq's government 1953

Iran's income from oil sales dwindled but Mossadeq remained hugely popular for standing up to the West and asserting Iran's independence. Meanwhile, the British tried to persuade the USA to join them in overthrowing Mossadeq. They did this by emphasising the Soviet threat to Iran and playing on America's fear that the Soviet Union might extend its influence into Iran and even get its hands on Iran's oil. After all, this was at the height of the Cold War and Iran had a long border with Soviet Russia. Eventually, in 1953, the Americans were convinced of the need to topple Mossadeq. With British help, they used threats and money to pressurise the Shah into dismissing Mossadeq and replacing him with a more pro-Western Prime Minister. Mossadeq was put on trial and imprisoned while the Iranian parliament was closed down. Years later, an American government minister admitted the coup was a 'setback for democratic government' in Iran.

The Shah and the West

The USA was now the strongest Western power in the Middle East region. The US government persuaded the Anglo-Iranian Oil Company (now BP) to join a group of American, French and Dutch oil companies in return for a 40 per cent share in the oil profits of Iran. This group then reached agreement with the new National Iranian Oil Company to start production again.

The Shah's new government signed a treaty with the USA in 1955 and, a year later, joined Britain, Turkey and Iraq in the so-called Baghdad Pact (see page 67). For the West, the Shah was a useful ally in the Middle East: he was reliably anti-Soviet and he was the guardian of the West's oil supplies. He was a reformer too, and many Iranians benefited from his policies: he transferred some of Iran's land from the biggest landowners to poorer farmers; he also gave women the vote, increased the number of schools and raised literacy rates. The country grew rich on the income from the oil industry which the National Iranian Oil Company now controlled.

Opposition to the Shah

But the huge new wealth was only enjoyed by a minority: there was still a huge gap between the rich élite and the poor masses. Dependence on the non-Muslim West caused anger: street demonstrations often targeted banks, because of their close ties to Western companies, and cinemas which showed mostly foreign, often sexy, films. These were felt to be un-Islamic. In 1971, the Shah held a huge celebration of what he claimed was the 2500th anniversary of the Persian monarchy. Not only did few believe the claim but, at a cost of $330 million, it was seen as far too extravagant, especially in a country where millions struggled to feed themselves.

Also, there was much resentment of Iran's close alliance with the West through its membership of the Baghdad Pact. Many saw the Shah as a pawn of the USA. In the late 1970s, the increasing opposition to his regime was led by the Muslim religious leaders, the **mullahs**. In the mosques, especially at the Friday prayers, the mullahs criticised the wealth, luxury and corruption of the Shah and his supporters. They feared and hated his secret police who arrested, imprisoned and tortured thousands of the government's critics, including mullahs. They also attacked the pro-Western, pro-Israeli foreign policy of the government.

The Islamic Revolution 1979

The outstanding leader of the opposition was **Ayatollah** Khomeini. Like many other Muslim religious leaders, he had been forced into exile by the Shah's government. At first, in 1964, he went to Turkey, later Iraq and, finally, France. From here, his writings and speeches were smuggled into Iran. In 1978, there were huge strikes and demonstrations calling on the Shah to abdicate. Every time the Shah's army and police killed people in these protests, there followed even bigger demonstrations, often a million-strong in the capital, Tehran. In September 1978, the

Key question
Why was there so much opposition to the Shah?

Key terms

Mullah
The title given to some Muslim clergy.

Ayatollah
Among Shia Muslims, the Ayatollahs are the most senior scholars, experts in interpreting the Koran.

Key question
Why was the Iranian Revolution successful?

Key date
Iranian Revolution led by Ayatollah Khomeini: 1979

Key terms

Martial law
Military
government, with
ordinary law
suspended.

Koran
The holy book of
the Muslims which,
they believe,
contains the word
of God as conveyed
to the Prophet
Muhammad in the
seventh century AD.

government introduced **martial law** and, the next day, troops killed over 500 people in a massive demonstration against the government. In October, there was a wave of strikes which brought most industry, including oil production, to a halt.

By the end of 1978 some soldiers were refusing to fire on crowds and some even fraternised with them, especially conscripts and those who admired Khomeini and sympathised with the protestors. Meanwhile, the Shah's advisers assured him that he was still popular and that it was only a minority of agitators who were misleading people and causing the protests. Then, in January 1979, the Shah left Iran in order to receive treatment for cancer. He never returned. Instead, the 76-year-old Khomeini returned in triumph, amid huge celebrations, and declared an Islamic Revolution. The Shah's last Prime Minister fled the country and most of the army declared support for the revolution. A national referendum produced a large majority in favour of abolishing the monarchy and establishing an Islamic republic.

The establishment of an Islamic state

Despite the huge support for the Ayatollah, there were other groups competing for power in Iran. For instance, there was the Communist Party and there were middle-class liberals who wanted a Western-style democracy. But it was Ayatollah Khomeini's supporters, organised in the Islamic Republican Party, that came to dominate the parliament and to hold the key positions in the government. Although Khomeini was not President or Prime Minister, he held ultimate power as the 'supreme leader' of Shiite Iran. He had the final say in government and law-making. New laws, based on the **Koran**, were passed; education was purged of

Ayatollah Khomeini
(1902–89) was
popular for his
opposition to the
Shah and the Shah's
dependence on the
USA, for his simple
lifestyle and
language, and his
religious beliefs.

un-Islamic influences, women had to cover their heads in public while alcohol, Western pop music and most Western films were banned. There were also mass trials of the Shah's former supporters and many were executed.

Khomeini and his government were keen to spread the Islamic revolution to what they saw as the corrupt, un-Islamic regimes in other parts of the Muslim world. Above all, they denounced the ties which bound other states to the West. A popular slogan was: 'Neither East nor West, but an Islamic government.'

The storming of the US embassy, November 1979

The USA, the former ally of the Shah, was seen as the main enemy in Iran and came to be known as 'The Great Satan'. When the US government allowed the Shah into the USA to receive medical treatment in November 1979, militant Iranian students stormed the US embassy in Tehran, and took 50 of the American staff as hostages. The US government declared Iran to be an international 'outlaw'. Yet millions in the Muslim world, both Arab and non-Arab, admired Khomeini for standing up to the West. Khomeini also took up the cause of the Palestinians and invited Yasser Arafat to Iran, where he received a hero's welcome.

Meanwhile, neighbouring Iraq was a prime target for the export of the Islamic Revolution. It had a completely **secular** government and a growing religious opposition. It also had a large Shiite population, who were excluded from top positions in government. Khomeini accused the Iraq government of being 'atheist' and 'corrupt' and, in one of his broadcasts to the people of Iraq, he called on them to: 'Wake up and topple this corrupt regime in your Islamic country before it is too late.'

This was a direct challenge to the new President of Iraq, Saddam Hussein.

Secular
Not religious or spiritual: a secular state is one not based on religion.

Key term

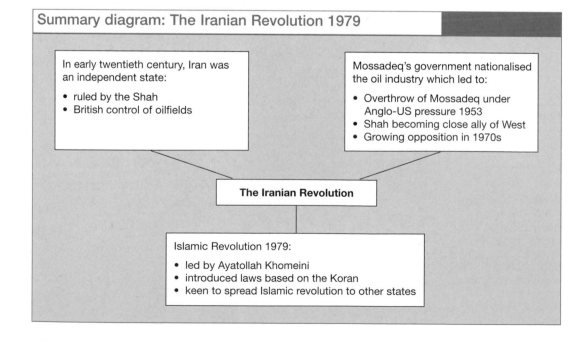

Summary diagram: The Iranian Revolution 1979

In early twentieth century, Iran was an independent state:
- ruled by the Shah
- British control of oilfields

Mossadeq's government nationalised the oil industry which led to:
- Overthrow of Mossadeq under Anglo-US pressure 1953
- Shah becoming close ally of West
- Growing opposition in 1970s

The Iranian Revolution

Islamic Revolution 1979:
- led by Ayatollah Khomeini
- introduced laws based on the Koran
- keen to spread Islamic revolution to other states

3 | The Iran–Iraq War 1980–8

Key question
What were Saddam Hussein's motives for invading Iran?

In 1980 Saddam Hussein went to war with Iran. He had many motives for attacking his neighbour:

- There was evidence of Iran's involvement in the assassination of leading members of the governing Baathist party in Iraq.

Key date
Iran–Iraq War: 1980–8

- There was an ongoing dispute about the border in the south: Iraq's access to the sea was very narrow while Iran had a long coastline and several ports through which it could export its oil. Iraq wanted to gain complete control of the Shatt al-Arab waterway (see the map on page 122) and thus gain a secure outlet to the sea. Saddam might even be able, perhaps, to claim part of oil-rich, south-west Iran.
- Now seemed the ideal time to attack: Iran's economy was in chaos following the fall of the Shah's regime; the country was facing a Western boycott of its trade because of the capture of the US embassy; and the Iranian armed forces were demoralised.
- Above all, however, it was fear of Iranian plots to overthrow him that motivated Saddam Hussein. If he could take advantage of Iran's weakness and defeat his neighbour in a short, quick war, he could strengthen his regime and also become the leading power in the oil-rich Gulf.

The course of the war 1980–8

Key question
Why was the war so prolonged?

When the Iraqi army invaded Iran in September 1980 there was little resistance and most observers felt that a short war was likely. Saddam himself called it the 'whirlwind war', confident that a swift, heavy blow would dislodge Khomeini's government. The Iraqis advanced far into Iran but, within a month, had been brought to a halt in the Iranian desert. They now resorted to firing missiles at Iran's cities in order to terrorise the civilian population. So began the so-called 'war of the cities' in which both sides bombed and killed hundreds of thousands of civilians.

Within a year, the Iraqis had been forced back to their own border. They had superior firepower but Iran, with its much bigger population, sent in waves of new recruits, hundreds of thousands, many of them fired up with revolutionary enthusiasm and willing to become **martyrs** for the Islamic Revolution. A reporter on the Iranian front wrote:

Key term
Martyr
Someone who dies or suffers greatly for a cause, especially for religious beliefs. There is a particularly strong tradition of martyrdom among Shiites.

> Religious slogans are posted everywhere, and sometimes reinforcements arrive cheerfully carrying their own coffins as a sign of willingness to be 'martyred'.

A message, left by one young Iranian soldier for his parents, was typical:

> Don't cry mother, because I am happy. I am not dead. Dear father, don't cry because you will be proud when you realise I am a martyr.

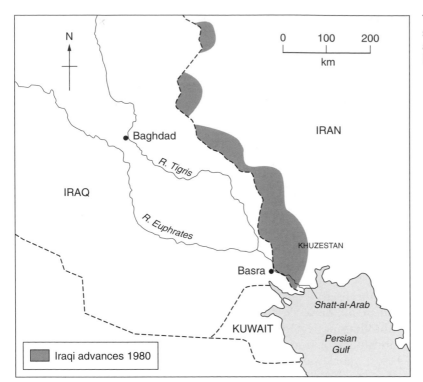

This map shows some of the main areas of fighting in the Iran–Iraq War.

Within two years Iran had recaptured all of its land and succeeded in cutting Iraq off from its sea ports. The war became prolonged and calls for a ceasefire came to nothing largely because Iran said it would not settle for anything less than the overthrow of Saddam's regime. When Iran stated that its target was Baghdad, the Iraqi capital, the Iraqi forces became more united in their determination to defend their country. By 1984, the two sides had become bogged down in trench warfare along the 1500-km border. It was similar, in this way, to the First World War fighting in the trenches except that sand, not mud, was what bogged the soldiers down.

Foreign involvement in the war

Another reason why the war lasted for so long was because of foreign involvement. Most of the Arab states supported Iraq. They feared that Iranian forces might cross the border to liberate the Iraqi Shiites and establish an Iraqi state loyal to Khomeini. They were opposed to the spread of Iran's revolutionary, Shiite version of an Islamic state. Although Khomeini appealed to *all* Muslims, the war certainly widened the Sunni/Shiite divisions.

In the Arab Gulf states which were closest to Iran (Kuwait, Qatar, Bahrain and the United Arab Emirates – see the map on page 116), there was little support for the Islamic Revolution except among the Shiite minority. The war also revived the historic animosity between Arabs and Persians. Saudi Arabia and the smaller oil-rich states in the Gulf, together with Egypt and Jordan, supported Iraq and supplied money and arms. Jordan

Key question
Which foreign powers became involved in the war?

also provided a vital route for Iraq's imports and exports through the port of Aqaba. This was essential for Iraq when its access to the Gulf was cut off by Iranian forces.

Syria, however, supported Iran because of intense rivalry with its neighbour, Iraq. The Syrians shut the Iraqi pipelines which passed through its territory to the Mediterranean. In return, Syria received free Iranian oil.

The USA was always more supportive of the Iraqis, as were France, Germany and the Soviet Union. They were all bitterly opposed to the new regime in Iran. The Soviet Union and France became the main suppliers of arms to Iraq. America's support became more active when the Iranians counterattacked and talked of advancing on Baghdad. The thought of the revolutionary Iranians controlling so much of the oil in the Gulf terrified the Americans as well as most of the Arab states. Khomeini might then be able to control world oil prices! And an Iranian victory might lead to the collapse of pro-Western regimes in the Gulf. Using their satellite technology, the Americans kept Iraq informed of Iranian troop movements. They also provided Iraq with equipment which was later used to make chemical weapons and, like the Arab states, they turned a blind eye when these were used against the Iranians.

Much of the war was focused on the Gulf, the vital route through which both Iraq and Iran exported their oil. The Iraqi air force controlled the skies but the Iranian navy was stronger. When the Iranians cut off Iraq's access to the Gulf through the Shatt al Arab waterway, the USA provided protection for Iraqi shipping and destroyed much of the Iranian navy.

Key question
What were the results
of the war?

The end of the war 1988

The Iranians finally accepted a ceasefire in 1988. Their economy was in ruins, the stream of 'martyrs' had subsided and they faced the prospect of a direct war with the USA. There was no peace treaty, only a truce, and both sides continued to re-arm. No one knows the exact figure of war dead but it is estimated that nearly a million Iranians and half a million Iraqis had died in the eight years of war. Although there had been a stalemate between the two sides for much of the war, there had been massive rocket attacks, by both sides, in the 'war of the cities' which led to huge civilian casualties and massive destruction. Brutality, on a huge scale, had been carried out by both sides. It had been one of the longest and most destructive wars since the Second World War.

Both sides had hoped that minority ethnic groups within the enemy country would rise up and welcome the invaders. The Iraqis had hoped that the Arab Sunni Muslims in the Khuzestan region of south-west Iran (see the map on page 122) would rise up and welcome their fellow Arab Sunnis from Iraq as liberators but that did not happen. Nor did the Shiites of southern Iraq join the advancing Shiite forces of Iran when they crossed the border into Iraq. National feelings (and loyalty to their rulers) proved stronger in both cases. No doubt terror played a part too: they feared what might happen to their families if they went over to the other side.

Khomeini said that agreeing to a ceasefire was a decision which he found 'more deadly than poison'. He died a year later in 1989. Despite eight years of warfare, in which hundreds of thousands had died, he was still revered by millions of Iranians for his proud, defiant stand after years of humiliation by stronger powers. Twelve million people filled the streets of Tehran for his funeral, lining the streets leading to the cemetery. The Islamic Republic continued to attract wide support in Iran.

Although Iran suffered massive destruction and loss of life, it had a population of 55 million and was still a major power. However, it had not succeeded in exporting its revolutionary, Shiite brand of Islam.

Iraq's economy and society had also suffered huge damage. Not only had half a million people been killed, but the health and education of the entire population suffered. During the war, more and more was spent on weapons (accounting for 93 per cent of all imports by 1984) so less and less was spent on hospitals and schools. Life expectancy fell and infant mortality increased. Yet, despite all the suffering in this long war, Iraq went to war again within two years.

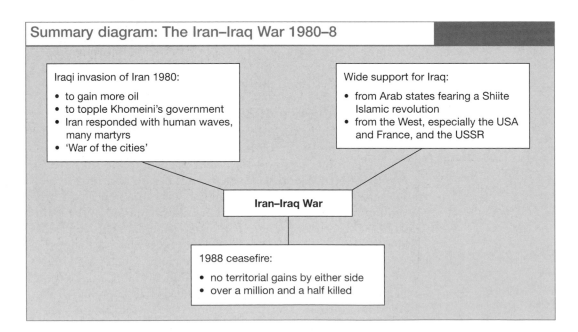

Summary diagram: The Iran–Iraq War 1980–8

Iraqi invasion of Iran 1980:

• to gain more oil
• to topple Khomeini's government
• Iran responded with human waves, many martyrs
• 'War of the cities'

Wide support for Iraq:

• from Arab states fearing a Shiite Islamic revolution
• from the West, especially the USA and France, and the USSR

Iran–Iraq War

1988 ceasefire:

• no territorial gains by either side
• over a million and a half killed

Study Guide

In the style of Edexcel and OCR

How far do you agree that the Iranian Revolution of 1979 accounts for both the outbreak, and the length of, the Iran–Iraq War of 1980–8?

Exam tips

The cross-references are intended to take you straight to the material that will help you to answer the question.

Start by re-reading pages 118–24 of this chapter.

There are two parts to this question: (a) the causes of the war and (b) reasons for its eight-year length. In evaluating the causal link in each part, you have to assess the importance of the Iranian Revolution relative to other factors.

(a) The causes of the war. Iraq attacked first, but why? Was it because of:
   • the threat which Iran's Shiite Islamic revolution posed to Saddam's secular, Arab government?
   • a dispute over boundaries and/or
   • a dispute over oil?
   • an opportunity to expand Iraq's territory when Iran was weak?

   Some of these factors, like the final one, may be linked to others, e.g. Iran may have been weaker as a result of the recent revolution. Explain these factors and any others you can think of.

(b) The reasons for the length of the war. You might examine and discuss some of the following questions in the light of the Iranian Revolution.
   • Why was it not the 'whirlwind war' that Saddam Hussein expected?
   • Why/how did trench warfare and the 'war of the cities' lengthen the conflict?
   • Why could not either side win a decisive victory?
   • Why did ceasefire calls come to nothing?
   • How did foreign intervention, from Arab states or from further afield, prolong the war? Again, what influence did the Iranian Revolution have (pages 122–3)?

In your conclusion, you need to weigh up how important the Iranian Revolution was, relative to other factors, in both causing and prolonging the war. Be clear and keep focused on showing causal links (or not) and assessing their significance.

8 Iraq and the West 1988–2008

POINTS TO CONSIDER

Despite suffering massive destruction and losing half a million lives in the war with Iran that ended in 1988, Saddam Hussein led his country to war again in 1990–1. This time, and then again in 2003, he found himself at war with the West, in particular with the USA, the superpower that now dominated the Middle East. Saddam's government was overthrown in 2003 yet liberation was to lead to foreign occupation and chaos. These developments are covered in this chapter under the following headings:

- Iraq, Kuwait and the Gulf War 1990–1
- The UN, the USA and the invasion of Iraq 2003
- Occupation, chaos and reconstruction in Iraq 2003–8

Key dates

1988		Iraqi forces attacked Halabja with chemical weapons
1990	August	Iraqi invasion of Kuwait
1991	Jan–March	First Gulf War
2000		Election of George W. Bush as US President
2001		Attack on the World Trade Center in New York
2002		Return of UN weapons inspectors to Iraq
2003		Invasion of Iraq – the Second Gulf War

1 | Iraq, Kuwait and the Gulf War 1990–1

Saddam Hussein and the Kurds

When the war with Iran ended in 1988, the Iraqi government promised the people peace and prosperity. What they got was further hardship and more terror. Instead of rebuilding Iraq, Saddam kept a million men in arms and poured money into developing the most advanced weapons. Against whom did he plan to use them? His immediate enemies were inside Iraq.

The Kurds form about 20 per cent of the population of Iraq. They are Muslims but not Arab and they speak a different

Key question
What was Saddam's 'Kurdish problem' and how did he solve it?

language. They are mostly situated in the north, especially along the borders with Syria, Turkey and Iran (see the map on page 116). There are millions of Kurds inside these neighbouring countries as well as in Iraq itself. However, the Iraqi Kurds were probably the most organised. Ever since the state of Iraq was created in 1921, the Kurds enjoyed a certain amount of autonomy or self-rule, but many of their leaders were determined to achieve a separate homeland, Kurdistan. There had been almost constant conflict between Iraqi troops and Kurdish nationalist fighters since the state of Iraq had been created.

During the 1970s, the Iranian government assisted the Iraqi Kurds in their struggle. They did this in order to weaken the state of Iraq which they saw as a rival. When Iran and Iraq went to war in 1980, this aid was increased and some of the Kurdish nationalist forces supported Iran. The Kurdish fighters often planned their attacks against Iraqi forces, in co-ordination with the Iranians, so as to coincide with Iranian offensives. In this way, they gained more control over the Kurdish north of Iraq. Not surprisingly, the Iraqi government of Saddam Hussein felt they were being stabbed in the back by their own people.

In 1988 the Iraqi forces took their revenge. Their planes bombarded the Kurdish town of Halabja, in northern Iraq, with chemical weapons. Five thousand people were killed immediately; 12,000 are estimated to have died later. One reporter wrote:

> Dead bodies – human and animal – littered the streets, huddled in doorways, slumped over the steering wheels of their cars. Survivors stumbled around, laughing hysterically, before collapsing. Those who had been directly exposed to the gas found that their symptoms worsened as the night wore on. Many children died along the way and were abandoned where they fell.
> (Quoted in D. McDowall, *A Modern History of the Kurds*, 2004.)

This was one of the episodes for which Saddam Hussein was later put on trial, found guilty and executed.

Saddam's solution to the 'Kurdish problem'

When the war with Iran ended in 1988, Saddam decided to solve the 'Kurdish problem' once and for all. He set out to depopulate much of the Kurdish north and destroy the Kurdish nationalist movement. His cousin, later nicknamed 'Chemical Ali' by the Kurds, was put in charge. Among the many documents and recordings later captured by the Americans, there is one recording in which he is heard saying to government officials: 'I will kill them all with chemical weapons! Who is going to say anything? The international community? F— them!'

Helicopters flew in low to kill all living things, animal as well as human, using a variety of chemical weapons. Where ground troops were used, Kurdish men aged 15–50 years were targeted: they were rounded up, shot and pushed into pre-dug graves. More than 100,000 refugees poured over the border, mostly into Turkey. Bulldozers flattened whole villages. About 180,000 were

Key date

Iraqi forces attacked Halabja with chemical weapons: 1988

killed in the campaign. Several towns and 90 per cent of all villages were destroyed. Millions of land mines were planted, especially in the border areas.

Discontent and unrest in Iraq

Even after a long war with Iran and despite huge debts, Saddam continued to build up his military machine and develop the most modern weapons. Yet the economy was in tatters and there was no post-war recovery: the value of Iraq's oil exports had declined because of war damage and a fall in the oil prices on the world market. Many people in the oil industry lost their jobs and, to make matters worse, thousands of soldiers were demobilised, thus adding to mounting unemployment.

Despite the terror exercised by Saddam's police and army, there were riots and strikes, some co-ordinated in the mosques which were beyond the control of Saddam's police and army. The army would not dare to attack the mosques, the most holy places, because it would intensify the opposition of all Muslims. But the main threat to Saddam came from his army. Many officers felt cheated of victory over Iran and some privately blamed Saddam for the failure to defeat their neighbour. There were several attempts to overthrow him between 1988 and 1990 and many officers were executed for conspiracy. Saddam needed to divert attention away from a growing military crisis in Baghdad. This may have been one of the reasons for the invasion of Kuwait.

Key question
Why was there discontent in Iraq?

The question of Kuwait

In the early twentieth century Kuwait was a small, insignificant fishing village at the southern end of the Turkish empire (see the map on page 131). The Turks planned to make it part of the Turkish province of Basra but the British intervened and signed a treaty with the main tribal leader to protect the independence of Kuwait. After the First World War and the defeat of Turkey, the British decided on, and then imposed, the borders of Iraq. These excluded Kuwait from Iraq.

The new Iraqi government refused to recognise the border with Kuwait, claiming that Iraq needed a safe outlet to the sea and that there were historic ties between Kuwait and Basra. In fact, many Kuwaitis had trade links with Basra and owned property there: for instance, the ruler of Kuwait, the Emir, owned more property in Basra than in Kuwait itself. Furthermore, many Kuwaitis wanted to be part of Iraq. They felt that they would be more secure as part of a wealthier, stronger country, especially as they feared their big Saudi neighbour. But then oil was discovered in Kuwait and neither the Kuwaitis nor their British protectors wanted to share it.

In the early 1960s, when the British recognised the full independence of Kuwait and planned to remove their troops, Iraq declared that Kuwait was a part of their country and claimed supreme power over it. The Arab League decided to send troops to protect Kuwait. In 1963, Iraq recognised Kuwait's independence but there continued to be tensions over the border.

Key question
Why did Saddam Hussein invade Kuwait?

United Nations Security Council
The most important body in the UN, it can take action against a country either by imposing sanctions or by using UN troops.

Trade sanctions
A form of punishment where the UN bans a country from trading with other countries in order to force it to obey a UN resolution.

Key question
What was the international response to Saddam's invasion?

Iraqi invasion of Kuwait: August 1990

In 1990, when oil prices on the world market dropped steeply, Saddam blamed Kuwait (and the United Arab Emirates) for deliberately causing the fall in prices by overproduction. He accused the Kuwaitis of doing this in order to undermine the Iraqi economy. He was also angry that Kuwait was pressing Iraq to repay the $14 billion it had lent to Iraq during the war with Iran. Saddam stressed that the Iraqi people had made huge sacrifices, in fighting Iran, thus protecting countries like Kuwait. Many Iraqis felt the same way: they felt that they had suffered in order to protect an ungrateful Arab world against the threat of Iranian expansionism. One Iraqi student said:

> The Kuwaitis boast of their aid to Iraq [during the war against Iran], but it was Iraq that defended their thrones and wealth with blood. We sacrificed our brothers, fathers and sons to let them enjoy life.

Saddam now demanded that Kuwait's border with Iraq should be adjusted and that Kuwait should make a further large loan to Iraq. He also accused Kuwait of drilling below the border with Iraq in order to extract huge oil deposits which Iraq claimed as its own.

Saddam's invasion of Kuwait, August 1990

With rising discontent at home and a military crisis on his hands, Saddam decided to invade Kuwait. In August 1990 a huge force of 300,000 crossed into Kuwait and overran the country. It took just three days and the rest of the world was completely surprised. However, the international reaction was almost unanimous. The **United Nations Security Council** agreed on complete **trade sanctions** against Iraq: no country was to have any trade with Iraq until their forces had withdrawn from Kuwait. These were the most complete and effective sanctions ever imposed by the UN.

Saddam, however, was defiant. He even announced that Kuwait had been annexed and become a province of Iraq. He also tried to win Arab support by saying that he would withdraw Iraqi forces only when the Israelis withdrew *their* forces from the West Bank and Gaza. The Palestinians were thrilled and many in Jordan were sympathetic but the majority of Arab states were united in condemning Iraq. When Saddam ordered the detention of hundreds of foreigners as hostages, mostly Westerners caught in Iraq or Kuwait, there was outrage. Some of the hostages were used as human shields by being kept near to military targets. Although the women and children, the sick and the old were soon released, there was still widespread condemnation of Iraqi behaviour. Then news emerged of atrocities committed by Iraqi troops on Kuwaiti citizens.

No one was more horrified at the Iraqi invasion of Kuwait than the Americans. As long ago as 1957, US President Eisenhower had written to one of his advisers: 'Should a crisis arise threatening to cut the Western world off from the Mid East oil, we would *have* to use force.'

When Iraqi forces massed on Kuwait's border with Saudi Arabia, many feared that Iraq might seize the Saudi oilfields, the biggest in the world, and thus gain control of more than half of the world's oilfields. When the King of Saudi Arabia requested that the USA send military forces to defend his country in case of attack, the Americans were quick to oblige. Over a period of a few months, there was a build-up of naval, land and air forces.

Although some Arab states, like Jordan, preferred an 'Arab' solution to the problem, the majority fully supported the deadline which the UN delivered to Iraq: withdraw from Kuwait by 15 January 1991 or face military force.

Saddam predicted the 'mother of all battles' and it started when the USA led a coalition of 34 countries into action. About 600,000 troops had been assembled in the deserts of Saudi Arabia. Most were American but Britain and France also sent large forces. Most significant of all was that many Arab countries such as Egypt and Syria sent troops, as did other Muslim countries such as Pakistan and Bangladesh. Saddam would not be able to claim that this was a Western crusade against the Arabs and Islam.

The Gulf War, January–March 1991

The war to liberate Kuwait became known as the Gulf War as Kuwait was situated at the head of the Persian Gulf (see the map on page 131). The fighting started with an air assault, largely by US forces, on Iraq in January 1991. The targets were not just military ones but airports, bridges, factories and roads. The aerial bombardment lasted five weeks. Saddam dug in, hoping world opinion would turn against the war. His forces fired Scud missiles into Israel in the hope that this would cause a split between the West and their Arab allies. The US persuaded the Israelis not to retaliate and the Arab members of the US-led coalition stayed firm.

In February the ground attack began. The Iraqis were driven out of Kuwait but not before they had torched the oil wells, causing a huge ecological disaster in the Gulf. Then US-led forces entered Iraq. The US President called on the Kurds in the north and the Shiites in the south to rise up and overthrow Saddam. They both responded, but they lacked arms and received no support from coalition forces. In the Shia south about 50,000 were killed by Saddam's forces and similar reprisals were expected in the Kurdish north. However, media coverage rallied world opinion and forced the USA and Britain to act. The Americans and British established **'no-fly zones'**, which prevented Saddam regaining control of the north. A 'safe haven' was created for the Kurds who have been effectively in control of their areas ever since.

Key question
What was the outcome of the Gulf War?

Key date
First Gulf War: January–March 1991

Key term
'No-fly zones'
These were areas in the Kurdish north and, later, the Shiite south where Iraqi planes were forbidden to fly. They were designed to protect these areas from attack by Saddam's army. The zones were policed by US and British planes which flew from bases in Turkey or from aircraft carriers in the Gulf.

This map shows the latitude lines, the 36th and 32nd parallels, that mark the north and south 'no-fly' zones. North of the 36th parallel was the mainly Kurdish area and south of the 32nd parallel was the mainly Shia area.

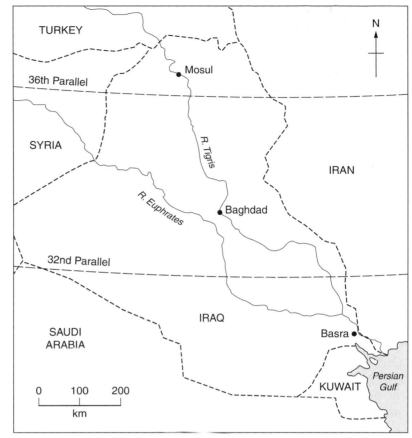

Ceasefire, March 1991

The coalition forces stopped short of Baghdad. Their UN mission had been restricted to the liberation of Kuwait and the USA's Arab allies would not have supported an American overthrow of Saddam. The coalition would have split if the Americans had attacked Baghdad. Instead, a ceasefire was called in March and peace terms were imposed on Iraq by the UN. These included:

- recognition of Kuwait's sovereignty
- payment of reparations (war damages)
- imposition of 'no-fly zones' in the Kurdish north and the south (and, for the next 12 years, US and British planes flew over these areas preventing the Iraqi air force from doing so)
- Iraqi co-operation with the UN to uncover and destroy all potential for producing **weapons of mass destruction (WMD)** whether biological, chemical or nuclear
- agreement with wide-ranging trade sanctions (which virtually cut off Iraq from the rest of the world) which were to last until all WMD were destroyed.

Key term

Weapons of mass destruction (WMD) Biological, chemical or nuclear weapons, used to kill as many people as possible.

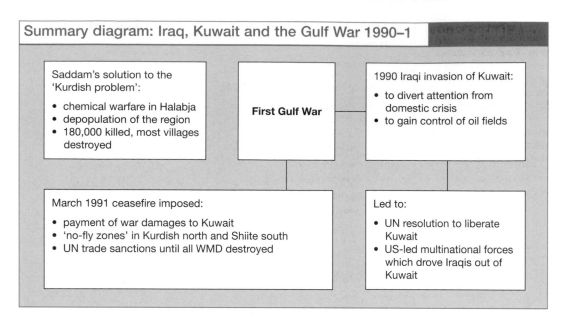

Summary diagram: Iraq, Kuwait and the Gulf War 1990–1

Saddam's solution to the 'Kurdish problem':

- chemical warfare in Halabja
- depopulation of the region
- 180,000 killed, most villages destroyed

First Gulf War

1990 Iraqi invasion of Kuwait:

- to divert attention from domestic crisis
- to gain control of oil fields

March 1991 ceasefire imposed:

- payment of war damages to Kuwait
- 'no-fly zones' in Kurdish north and Shiite south
- UN trade sanctions until all WMD destroyed

Led to:

- UN resolution to liberate Kuwait
- US-led multinational forces which drove Iraqis out of Kuwait

2 | The UN, the USA and the Invasion of Iraq 2003

The search for weapons of mass destruction

One month after the ceasefire, the UN formed a special committee (**UNSCOM**) to search for and destroy Iraq's WMD. Until all those weapons had been destroyed, trade sanctions would be imposed on Iraq. A wide variety of imports were banned. At first, this pressure worked: Iraq co-operated and admitted that it had stockpiled nerve gas and chemical warheads while the UN inspectors uncovered a nuclear programme with several kilograms of highly enriched uranium, necessary for the production of nuclear weapons.

After a year UNSCOM declared that it had destroyed all medium- and long-range missiles and, three years later, that it had destroyed all the material for making nuclear and chemical weapons. However, it had not been able to eliminate all of Iraq's biological weapons programme. Nevertheless, by 1995, the Iraqi government was confident that sanctions would soon be lifted and confessed to the production of some anthrax and nerve gas while claiming that the stockpiles had been destroyed during the Gulf War. UNSCOM demanded proof but this was not forthcoming.

At this time, Saddam's son-in-law, who had fallen out of favour with Saddam because of a family feud, defected to Jordan. He told those who questioned him in Jordan that, after the Gulf War, Saddam's second son had been given the job of hiding Iraq's WMD. (He was later promised a pardon by Saddam and returned to Baghdad, only to be shot three days later. His uncle said: 'We have cut off the treacherous branch from our noble family tree'.) The Americans were now increasingly suspicious and distrustful of the Iraqi government and they began to demand **'regime change'**

Key question
What evidence of WMD did UN inspectors find?

UNSCOM
UN special committee set up to search for and destroy Iraq's WMD.

'Regime change'
Change in the system of government (in this case, Saddam's dictatorship).

Key terms

(i.e. the removal of Saddam) before they would agree to the lifting of sanctions.

Key question
How did Iraq survive UN sanctions?

The impact of sanctions on Iraq

From the end of the war in 1991, Iraq was subjected to a blockade which prevented it from importing machinery, fertilisers, most medicines and even books. At first Iraq was not allowed to sell oil and, even when this ban was lifted after a few months, Iraq was still allowed to sell only a small amount of oil. As a result, the country could afford only very modest food imports and, in a country which had been importing 70 per cent of its food, this had disastrous consequences. Sanctions led to hardship and poverty on a massive scale. Malnutrition and a huge rise in infant mortality were reported. A UN survey in the mid-1990s claimed that, in the Baghdad area, a quarter of those under the age of five years old were 'severely malnourished' (a higher proportion than in most African states) and, by 1997, 7000 children were dying each month of hunger and disease.

The bombing of electricity plants in the war had led to a breakdown of the water purification systems, yet Iraq was not allowed to import chlorine as a water disinfectant for fear it might be a source of the chlorine gas used in chemical weapons. The contamination of water led to widespread outbreaks of dysentery. It is reckoned that between a quarter and half a million children died as a result of sanctions and Saddam's rule. As the humanitarian crisis worsened, the UN came up with a plan in 1996 to allow Iraq to sell its oil in order to buy food. This 'Oil for Food' programme was to be run by the UN. It brought much-needed relief to a desperate people.

Yet sanctions did not increase the opposition to Saddam's regime in Iraq, let alone lead to rebellion. Instead, they led to a widespread feeling of hopelessness while the rationing of food meant that the government could control who received food and thus ensure that the regime's key supporters were given priority. Saddam used violence and terror, as ever, to control resources and reward his most loyal supporters. Disloyal elements in the army were purged, sometimes executed. A special army unit was created to protect the President and nearly all the top jobs in government and the armed forces went to Sunnis, particularly to members of Saddam's own family and tribe.

The roads, bridges and electricity systems in Baghdad and the Sunni areas were largely rebuilt and, although Iraq's WMD programme was depleted, the army was still the biggest in the Arab world. Meanwhile Saddam allowed the filming of mass suffering, especially for Arab television networks, so that the image of Iraq as the victim of the greedy, uncaring West would be propagated. International opinion turned against the continuation of sanctions.

Iraq fights back and emerges from isolation

Saddam did not want to give up all his secret weapons and had always tried to disrupt the UN weapons inspectors. Besides, he knew that the inspection teams were working closely with the **CIA** and other Western intelligence agencies. He no doubt suspected that they were planning to overthrow him. In 1996, the new, Australian leader of the UNSCOM inspection team demanded access, with no advance warning given, to the headquarters of the special security services and to the presidential palaces. Saddam refused and, in 1997, the UNSCOM inspectors were forced to leave Iraq. A year later, in 1998, American (and British) planes started bombing Iraqi military sites despite the commonly held view that Iraq had no more WMD.

Most Arab states had been happy to see Iraq taught a lesson in 1991 but now the bombing campaign turned many of them against the USA. When the US Secretary of State Madeleine Albright was asked on television if the starvation of half a million people was justified, she said it had been 'worth it'. This caused widespread anger in the Arab world and several states started to trade with Iraq again. Saudi Arabia and Kuwait still provided the US with bases from which to launch bombing raids on Iraq but there was an increasing amount of oil smuggling across Iraq's borders with Syria, Iran and Turkey, which the UN could not control. Iraq was re-emerging from international isolation.

Even the USA seemed to accept the revival of Iraq's oil industry. A growing global economy was pushing up oil prices and several American firms won contracts to rebuild Iraq's oil wells. By 1999 the UN had approved unlimited oil exports from Iraq and Saddam's regime had restored diplomatic relations with all its neighbours. It had got rid of the hated UN inspectors and still had the most feared army in the Arab world. Saddam had challenged the UN, and the world's one and only superpower, and had survived. When George W. Bush was elected President of the USA in 2000, there was renewed talk in Washington of the need to 'remove Saddam'.

Background to invasion

Ten years after the First Gulf War, Saddam Hussein was still defiant and still in control of the country with the world's second largest oil reserves. Many members of the new US government regretted that American forces had not removed Saddam in 1991. They believed he was a threat to the whole region and, in particular, to US interests in the Middle East. Plans for an invasion were drawn up: now that Iraq was weakened by sanctions, it would put up less resistance while there was no rival superpower to check the USA or come to Iraq's defence. Then, in September 2001, came the attack on the World Trade Center in New York and the Pentagon in Washington and the US diverted its attention to Afghanistan (see pages 148–9).

Key question
How did Iraq emerge from international isolation?

Key dates

Election of George W. Bush as US President: 2000

Attack on the World Trade Center in New York: 2001

Key term

CIA
The US Central Intelligence Agency, responsible for gathering information about foreign governments for the US government.

Key question
Why did the USA launch an invasion of Iraq in 2003?

Profile: Saddam Hussein 1937–2006

1937	– Born into a poor peasant family in Takrit, near Baghdad
1957	– Became a Baath Party activist
1963	– Became head of the Iraqi Intelligence Services
1968–79	– Vice-President of Iraq
1979	– Became President of Iraq
1980–8	– War with Iran
1990	– Invasion of Kuwait
1991	– Iraq defeated by US-led coalition and UN sanctions imposed
2003	– US-led invasion led to end of Saddam's regime and later capture
2004–6	– Trial and execution for crimes against humanity

Saddam was brought up by his uncle and, as a young man, was immersed in the anti-British, anti-Western atmosphere of the Arab world in the late 1950s and the 1960s. He was involved in the overthrow of the pro-British monarchy in 1958. In the 1960s and 1970s, he emerged as the strong man of the Iraqi regime, establishing control over the security services and, later, the army. He oversaw the nationalisation of Iraq's oil industry in 1972 and used Iraq's oil wealth to build up education, health and welfare services that were among the best in the Arab world.

As President, Saddam was ruthless in eliminating his rivals and, like Stalin whom he admired, he used 'show trials' of his enemies to enforce submission to his rule. Many of his closest advisers came from the same Takrit clan as he did and several members of his close family, including his two sons, held important posts in government.

Saddam's eight-year war with Iran, which ended in 1988, led to stalemate, huge debt and a shattered economy. Yet two years later, his army invaded Kuwait, claiming that the country belonged to Iraq. Defeat by US-led forces and the imposition of UN sanctions were to weaken Iraq and bring misery to the people, yet Saddam remained defiant. His propaganda machine portrayed him as the father-figure and protector of his people while he continued to have his opponents, including two sons-in-law, murdered.

In 2003, the USA and its allies launched an invasion, claiming that Iraq still had WMD, and overthrew Saddam's regime. Saddam escaped and went into hiding but was captured by US troops in December 2003. After a two-year trial he was sentenced, by an Iraqi court, to death by hanging, a sentence that was carried out in December 2006.

At the start of 2002 President Bush still had his sights on Iraq. He accused the country of being part of **'the axis of evil'**, alongside Iran and North Korea. The USA claimed that Iraq still had WMD and feared that **al-Qaida** might get its hands on them. There was no evidence of any link between al-Qaida and Iraq, but the USA seemed set on invading Iraq. It now had to convince public opinion that invasion would be legitimate. That meant convincing the world that Iraq still had WMD. The US government persuaded the UN to call for the return of weapons inspectors to Iraq and to threaten Iraq with 'serious consequences' if it was obstructive. As the USA built up its forces in the Gulf, Iraq complied. Several months later, the UN team reported that they had found no evidence of WMD.

However, it was now clear that the USA had made up its mind on invasion in order to topple Saddam. The US government still sought UN approval for going to war but Britain was the only one of the other four permanent members of the UN Security Council to support a UN resolution in support of invasion: Russia, China and France were all opposed. In Britain, the Prime Minister, Tony Blair, prepared to take Britain to war in Iraq despite widespread opposition. He claimed that Iraq still had WMD and that some of them could 'be ready within 45 minutes of an order to use them'. Thus, said Blair, Iraq posed a huge threat to peace and stability in the Middle East. Russia, China and France all called for the UN inspectors to have more time to continue their work.

The invasion of Iraq, March 2003

The US and British governments did not have the authority of a UN resolution to go to war as they had done in the 1991 war. The forces that invaded Iraq in March 2003 constituted what the US President called 'the coalition of the willing'. The coalition forces were largely made up of American troops, with several thousand British and small contingents from Australia and Poland. It was nothing like the truly multinational force that had driven the Iraqis out of Kuwait in 1991.

As in 1991 the war started with aerial bombardment followed by invasion on land. There was very little Iraqi resistance: many Iraqi troops just melted away. Most Iraqi people remained neutral, not willing to risk their lives to save Saddam's government. There was no great battle for Baghdad, which had already been pounded by American planes, and the capital fell to the Americans after three weeks. British forces took control of Basra, in the south. The Kurds remained in control of their area in the north, as they had done since the 'no-fly zones' were established in 1991. On 1 May 2003 President Bush declared that the war was over. Little did he realise how long the peace would take.

Key terms

'The axis of evil'
A phrase used by US President Bush to describe the link he saw between the states that he regarded as enemies.

Al-Qaida
From the Arabic word meaning a base (e.g. for training recruits in Afghanistan), it came to refer to an organisation, or a network, of Islamists of whom Osama Bin Laden was the leader. Responsible for the attacks on New York and Washington in 2001.

Key dates

Return of UN weapons inspectors to Iraq: 2002

Invasion of Iraq – the Second Gulf War: 2003

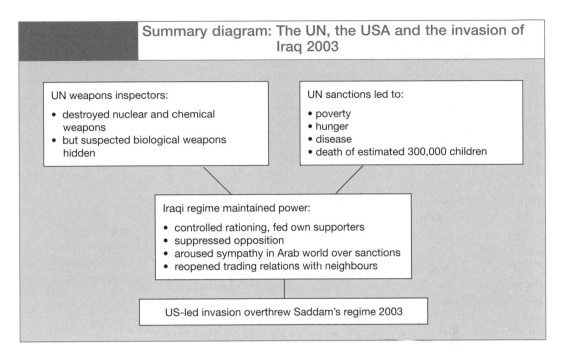

Summary diagram: The UN, the USA and the invasion of Iraq 2003

UN weapons inspectors:
- destroyed nuclear and chemical weapons
- but suspected biological weapons hidden

UN sanctions led to:
- poverty
- hunger
- disease
- death of estimated 300,000 children

Iraqi regime maintained power:
- controlled rationing, fed own supporters
- suppressed opposition
- aroused sympathy in Arab world over sanctions
- reopened trading relations with neighbours

US-led invasion overthrew Saddam's regime 2003

Key question
Why did the occupation of Iraq descend into chaos?

3 | Occupation, Chaos and Reconstruction in Iraq 2003–8

The US forces put the oilfields under military guard and also took control of key government buildings. They also scoured the country for WMD, but none were ever found. Unfortunately, they had given little thought to how they would govern Iraq. After many years of repression and brutality under Saddam and further suffering caused by sanctions, the country now descended into chaos.

Looting breaks out

In Baghdad poor people broke into government buildings having heard rumours of food stockpiled there. Then looting broke out on a massive scale: not just food stores but banks, hospitals, universities and the homes of leading members of the fallen government were ransacked. Similar scenes were enacted in other cities. There were little more than 150,000 coalition forces in a country of 26 million people. They were not prepared for the role of policing and they were not able to control the looting. Many Iraqi cities experienced a complete breakdown of law and order and, for millions of Iraqis, the quality of daily life deteriorated. Services such as water, sewage disposal and electricity, which had been poor during the sanctions regime under Saddam, became even worse. Ordinary Iraqis became angry with the occupying forces for not providing basic law and order. Meanwhile organised gangs took control of the looting and a resistance movement emerged.

Resistance

Resistance to the occupying forces started almost immediately. It often began with demonstrations calling for jobs or basic services like water and electricity. When things got out of control, US forces fired on the crowds. Then, when the Americans set up a temporary government, the **Coalition Provisional Authority** (CPA), they decided to abolish Saddam's army: suddenly, 350,000 soldiers were demobilised. They lost their salaries but kept their guns. Many joined the resistance. From 2004 onwards, the number of attacks on US forces increased. There were reckoned to be about 20,000–50,000 actively involved in the **insurgency**, as the armed resistance to the American occupation came to be known. There were many different groups involved, about 10 per cent of whom were thought to be non-Iraqi, some linked to al-Qaida.

Very few American forces spoke Arabic and they knew little of the customs of Iraq. Uncertain of who was friend and who was foe, the Americans struggled to restore law and order, let alone relieve the daily suffering of millions of Iraqis. As they rounded up hundreds, and then thousands, of suspects, they reopened the hated Abu Ghraib prison where so many Iraqis had been imprisoned and tortured under Saddam. Then, in 2004, it emerged that Americans themselves had been subjecting the inmates to their own form of humiliation and torture. A small number of American troops had taken photographs of the treatment of Iraqi prisoners: the worst of these showed naked prisoners forced to perform sex acts with each other or having electric cables attached to their arms, legs and genitals. Another showed a naked Iraqi prisoner, with a leash tied round his neck, being pulled along, like a dog, by a female American soldier. Only a few of the US troops were guilty but the publicity, both in Iraq and around the world, fuelled the resistance and did great damage to America's reputation.

Key terms

Coalition Provisional Authority
An organisation set up by the USA and its coalition allies to govern Iraq.

Insurgency
An uprising to try and overthrow a government.

Reconstructing Iraq

Most of the members of the American-led CPA had little experience of rebuilding a national economy, let alone rebuilding a whole nation. However, their overriding concern was with dealing with the insurgency. While they concentrated on defeating the insurgency, the rebuilding of Iraq (e.g. repairing water, sewage and electricity systems) was neglected. Yet only when they were seen to be rebuilding the country and restoring essential services would they win the popular support needed to defeat the insurgents. It was a vicious circle and the insurgents knew it: they deliberately bombed water, sewage and electricity facilities, as well as US troops, in order to make the occupation unworkable.

Meanwhile, the US forces began to build and train a new Iraqi army and a police force but the new recruits became targets for the insurgents. At least 3000 Iraqi soldiers or police officers were killed by suicide bombers between 2003 and 2008. Anyone who

Key question
What were the difficulties of reconstruction?

co-operated with the Americans was seen, by the insurgents, as collaborating with the enemy. Suicide bombings and kidnappings became daily occurrences. Some of those kidnapped were foreigners, especially Americans and British, but most were Iraqis, often taken captive so that large sums of money could be extracted as ransom payments.

In the north of the country the Kurdish forces kept control and maintained law and order. Reconstruction could proceed in this more secure situation. The oil wells increased their production and foreign companies invested in the development of the region. In the rest of Iraq, however, there was continuing lawlessness. In 2005 the Americans and their Iraqi allies in the government organised national elections. Most people voted along sectarian lines, i.e. for parties that represented their particular ethnic, usually religious, group or sect. As the Shiites made up 60 per cent of the population, most of their votes went to Shiite parties who thus won most of the seats in the Iraqi parliament.

The Sunni insurgency

Despite this democratic development the violence continued. The Sunnis, in particular, were prominent in the insurgency. They feared domination by the Shia majority. They were also fearful because most of Iraq's oil was in the Kurdish north or Shiite south. They were afraid of losing their economic, as well as their political, power. In 2005–6 there were a number of attacks on Shiite mosques. These may have been carried out by Iraqi Sunnis who feared a Shiite-dominated Iraq. Equally, they may have been carried out by bombers sympathetic to al-Qaida as part of their campaign to drive the Americans out of the Middle East by causing maximum destruction. It was difficult to know who was responsible for all the bombing in an increasingly lawless and violent country. Either way, the bombing of Shiite mosques led to retaliation: there were several attacks on Sunni mosques as well as reports that Shiites in the Iraqi police force were murdering Sunnis.

Nevertheless, there were some improvements and the situation was not wholly bleak. The hated regime of Saddam Hussein had been overthrown and, in 2006, he was tried and later executed for **'crimes against humanity'**, such as the gassing of the Kurds in 1988 (see page 127). A parliament was elected in 2005, a new Iraqi-run government was established and the police and armed forces were built up. By 2008, the daily death toll had decreased and the Iraqi authorities had largely taken control of their country. However, they still depended on the support of American troops; millions of Iraqis were unemployed; crime was rife and the provision of basic services like water, sewage and electricity was patchy. The recovery of Iraq continues to be a long process.

Key term

'Crimes against humanity'
Widespread or systematic attack against a civilian population.

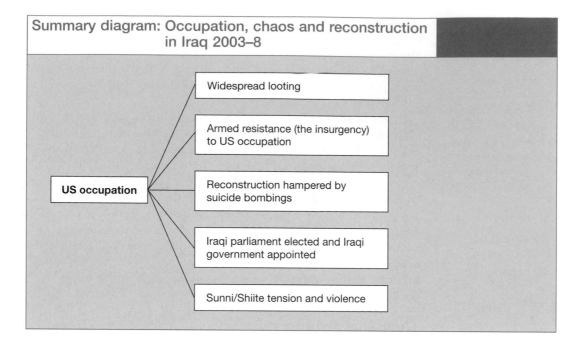

Summary diagram: Occupation, chaos and reconstruction in Iraq 2003–8

Study Guide

In the style of Edexcel and OCR

How far do you agree that Western powers intervened in Iraq from 1991 to 2003 in order to remove Saddam Hussein from power?

Exam tips

The cross-references are intended to take you straight to the material that will help you to answer the question.

It would be worth re-reading the whole of Chapter 8 first.

The period 1991–2003 starts with the war over Kuwait and ends with the invasion of Iraq. Your essay should focus on the reasons for Western involvement in these wars but it should also assess the motives for Western intervention in Iraq in the intervening years. Be alert to differences in policy among the Western powers and make space for them in your answer.

On the Kuwait War of 1991, you need to analyse:

- the reaction of the Western powers (e.g. USA and Europeans) to Iraq's invasion of Kuwait
- reasons for and extent of their involvement in the subsequent war
- the extent to which the Western powers were acting alone
- the extent to which their objective was purely to liberate Kuwait. Or to what extent their motivation was driven by the wish to protect their oil supplies and/or strengthen their ties with other Arab states and/or to topple Saddam (pages 129–31).

(Remember that motives may have been mixed as well as complex.)

In the years after the ceasefire of March 1991, leading up to the invasion of 2003, you should assess:

- aims and extent of the West's involvement:
  - in UN sanctions
  - in UN weapons inspection
  - in 'no-fly zones' in the 1990s
- how the success or failure of these measures led to invasion in 2003
- who invaded Iraq in 2003 and why
- whether the invasion was launched to rid Iraq of WMD or to topple Saddam's regime (pages 131–6).

In conclusion, you need to weigh up the importance, both for the US and for other Western powers, of driving Saddam from power in each of:

- the 1991 war
- the sanctions, weapons inspections and no-fly zones in the 1990s
- the invasion of 2003
- and overall as the fundamental motive of Western policy towards Iraq in the years from 1991 to 2003.

9 From Arab Nationalism to Islamic Fundamentalism

POINTS TO CONSIDER

From the late 1960s Arab nationalism lost its appeal and Islamic fundamentalism became a growing force in the Middle East. Al-Qaida emerged and later grew into a worldwide network of Islamic radicals. It achieved international notice in 2001 with its attacks on New York and Washington. This chapter examines:

- The rise of political Islam
- Al-Qaida and the globalisation of terror

Key dates

1967		Arabs defeated by Israel in Six-Day War
1979		Islamic Revolution in Iran
		Soviet invasion of Afghanistan
1990		Iraqi invasion of Kuwait
1990–1		US troops arrived in Saudi Arabia
2001	September	'9/11' attacks on New York and Washington
	October	US attack on Afghanistan
2003		US-led invasion of Iraq

1 | The Rise of Political Islam

When the Egyptian leader, Nasser, died in 1970, millions turned out for his funeral and he was mourned by many more millions throughout the Arab world. He had been a towering Arab leader, inspiring and exciting those who heard his speeches, whether at rallies or on the radio. He was the undisputed voice of Arab nationalism, the movement that united so much of the Arab world in its defiance of the West and Israel.

However, Arab nationalism was already on the wane when Nasser died. The main reason was the crushing defeat which the Arab nations of Egypt, Syria and Jordan suffered in their war against Israel in 1967 (see pages 50–3). In that war, the Israelis proved that they were stronger than the three Arab states put together and they seized land from all of them. Arab nationalism was seen to have failed and lost its appeal as a unifying force in the wake of the Arabs' humiliation at the hands of Israel and its

Key question
What gave rise to the growth of political Islam?

Key date
Arabs defeated by Israel in Six–Day War: 1967

Political Islam
A political movement which asserts that Islam is the solution to the problems of the modern world. Its followers advocate Islamic states where the Koran is the basis of government and society.

Islamic fundamentalism
The belief that the state should be based wholly on Islamic law, as in Muhammad's day.

Jihad
An Arabic word meaning 'struggle', both internal and personal (against sin) and external (against threats to Muslim lands).

Western backers, especially the USA. In the years ahead, the vacuum left by Arab nationalism was to be filled by radical or **political Islam**, sometimes called **Islamic fundamentalism**.

Political Islam or Islamic fundamentalism

At the heart of this movement was the belief that Muslims (and nearly all Arabs are Muslims) should return to their Islamic values and establish states based on laws derived from the Koran, the Muslim holy book. The followers of this radical, political Islam believed that, through Islam, they could best unify, strengthen and defend themselves against the military and economic power of the West. Israel, of course, was seen as part of the West, regarded as a foreign, non-Muslim state carved out of Arab lands by the West.

The followers of political Islam are sometimes called fundamentalists because they believe that the state should be based *wholly*, or fundamentally, on Islamic law, as in Muhammad's day, and all changes introduced from the West should be eliminated. In practice, it was unlikely that such a fundamentalist regime would ever be implemented: even the most radical or extreme Islamists have made use of Western inventions like the Internet, for example.

Arab nationalism had accepted the special place of Islam in the life of most Arabs but not in the political life of the nation. Arab nationalists put more stress on their common language, Arabic, and on their historical ties than they did on religion as a unifying force for the Arabs. Arab nationalism was, essentially, secular. By contrast, radical Islamic groups wanted no division between political and religious life, between religion and government. They stressed the importance of Islam in renewing their societies and enabling them to resist the domination of the West. Political Islam thrived, above all, because it was the most potent protest movement and was the first home-grown ideology in the Arab world. Many followers of political Islam believed in *jihad*, an Arabic word meaning 'struggle'. Its primary meaning, as used in the Koran, is the internal struggle against sin or bad habits (whether the personal struggle of the individual or that of the Islamic community). It is also used to mean the struggle to defend Muslim lands from external aggression.

Political Islam was not only a challenge to foreign, non-Muslim powers. It was also, like Arab nationalism, a challenge to the governments of Muslim countries. Several Arab countries, in particular, felt threatened, just as they had been by Arab nationalism. Again, the countries who felt most threatened were the more conservative monarchies like Saudi Arabia and Jordan and those with the closest ties to the West. Some of the smaller, oil-rich states in the Gulf, like Kuwait, were ruled by rich élites who did not wish to lose their power to the Muslim clergy. Egypt, under Nasser's successor, Anwar Sadat, also felt the pressure. This was particularly so after Sadat had made peace with Israel in 1978. He was seen to have broken the united front of Arab countries who refused to recognise the state of Israel and it was radical **Islamists** in the Egyptian army who assassinated Sadat in 1981.

The Islamic Revolution in Iran 1979

What did surprise many people, in both the Muslim and the wider world, was that when the Islamic revolution first occurred, it was not in an Arab country but in Iran. The government of the Shah of Iran had seemed so strong with its large, modern army and a brutal secret police. Yet the Iranian Revolution was both revolutionary and Islamic (see Chapter 7). The Shah was overthrown by a massive, popular movement and a republic based on Islamic law, with a religious figure, Ayatollah Khomeini, as its 'supreme leader', was established (pages 118–20). Furthermore, Khomeini and his fellow religious leaders proclaimed that the governments of other Muslim countries in the Middle East were corrupt, un-Islamic and deserved to be overthrown. They particularly criticised those countries with ties to the West or to the Soviet Union.

Although many millions of Arab Muslims applauded the Islamic Revolution in Iran, especially when the Iranians defied the USA by taking its diplomats hostage, their enthusiasm soon waned while the governments of most Arab states became highly suspicious of Iran. This was partly for historical reasons: Iran was Persian, not Arab. It was also partly for religious reasons: the people of Iran were mostly Shiite Muslims whereas the Arab Muslims were mostly Sunnis. When Iran found itself at war with Iraq in 1980, most Arab, Muslim states supported secular, Sunni-dominated, Arab Iraq (page 122).

Most Arab states did not want to embrace radical Islamic politics. For those Arabs who *did* want to see the spread of political Islam, it was Afghanistan (see map on page 116), to the east of Iran, that provided the focus for their energies after 1979.

The emergence of al-Qaida

In 1978, Afghan communists, supported by the Soviet Union, seized control of the government of their country. They immediately faced rebellion from a number of Islamist groups who resented the foreign, communist influence of their pro-Soviet government. In December 1979 the Soviet Union sent in troops to assist the government. This invasion led to a huge rebellion and, over the next 10 years, the Afghan guerrillas, or ***mujahideen***, were to fight the Soviet troops. The *mujahideen* were seen as patriots fighting for Afghan independence and they received massive support. Not only did Muslim countries like Saudi Arabia and neighbouring Pakistan (a Muslim country) provide support, but so too did the USA, Britain and other Western countries because they wanted to push back the Soviet forces and defeat the USSR. This was still the era of the Cold War and the West was keen to resist the advance of what the US President, Ronald Reagan, called the 'evil empire'.

Key question
What was the impact of the Iranian Revolution in the Arab world?

Key dates

Islamic Revolution in Iran: 1979

Soviet invasion of Afghanistan: 1979

Key terms

Islamists
Those who believe in political Islam.

Mujahideen
An Arabic word meaning 'those who struggle', for example in a *jihad*, or holy war.

Key question
Where and how did al-Qaida emerge?

The Western powers, especially the USA, provided much of the weaponry, including Stinger missiles to shoot down Soviet helicopter gunships, while countries like Saudi Arabia encouraged many volunteers to go and fight in Afghanistan. The military intelligence services of Pakistan, Saudi Arabia, the USA and Britain trained and armed recruits to fight against the Soviet forces. One of the Saudi volunteers was Osama Bin Laden. He was the son of the owner of a large construction business in Saudi Arabia and he used his wealth and expertise to build a vast underground complex for weapons and medical facilities in Afghanistan. He also took charge of an organisation which co-ordinated the activities of the thousands of Arab Islamists fighting alongside the Afghan *mujahideen* and he established training camps or bases, the Arabic word for which is *al-Qaida*. About 15,000 volunteers from Saudi Arabia trained in these camps and several thousand were trained in Egypt to go and fight in Afghanistan. These 'Arab Afghans' became battle-hardened, experienced guerrilla fighters.

In 1989 the Soviet forces were finally forced to withdraw from Afghanistan. They had faced fierce resistance and realised they were fighting a war they could not win. The war had lasted for 10 years and cost the lives of a million Afghans. It had given rise to the growth of numerous Islamist organisations and inspired millions to believe in their powers. Many Islamist groups felt that, if they could defeat the Soviet Union, then surely they could defeat their own much weaker, unpopular Arab regimes?

The growth of political Islam

Key question
How did Arab governments respond to political Islam?

In the Arab countries, those attracted to radical, political Islam were often young, angry, educated and middle class, like engineers, doctors and scientists. Their organisations were often banned by the authorities, their activities were monitored by the security services and many were arrested. However, they thrived in the one area which the Arab governments dared not ban – in the mosques. Sermons were recorded and spread via cassettes, later by CDs and the Internet. The Islamists often established education and welfare services that were better than those provided by the State. In this way, they often won wide support.

However, some of their terrorist activities caused outrage both at home and abroad. In Egypt there was an increasing number of attacks in the mid-1990s, mostly on police officers and government officials but also on Western tourists. These activities led to a clampdown by the government in which urban areas suspected of protecting the perpetrators were attacked by helicopters and troops. This in turn led to several assassination attempts on Egyptian President Mubarak. The killing of 58 tourists in one attack in 1997 led to the execution of 60 ringleaders and the detention without trial of 20,000 people. Egypt's militant Islamists were too weak to continue their campaign after this, but some of the Islamists' demands were met with the increasing adoption of the veil by women in public and of religious law in settling disputes over marriage and divorce.

During the war in Afghanistan, the 'Arab Afghans' had received huge support from the US and Saudi governments but this alliance was shattered by the US-led attack on Iraq after the invasion of Kuwait in 1990–1. The 'Arab Afghans' and other Islamists were alarmed that the Saudi government had invited US troops into Saudi Arabia. They were horrified to see 'the forces of unbelievers occupy Islamic soil'. They thought the presence of US forces, in the land of the Prophet Muhammad, defiled the holy shrines of Mecca and Medina and was an insult to Muslims everywhere. In the eyes of Osama Bin Laden, the Saudi authorities had forfeited their claim to protect Islam. He branded the Saudi rulers as renegades from Islam. In 1992, he left Saudi Arabia for the Sudan and, two years later, the Saudi authorities deprived him of his Saudi nationality so that he became stateless.

Iraqi invasion of
Kuwait: 1990

US troops arrived in
Saudi Arabia: 1990–1

Key dates

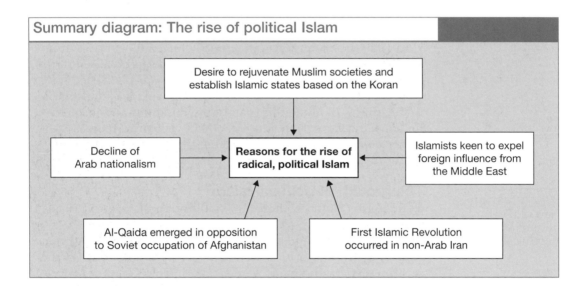

Summary diagram: The rise of political Islam

Desire to rejuvenate Muslim societies and establish Islamic states based on the Koran

Decline of Arab nationalism

Reasons for the rise of radical, political Islam

Islamists keen to expel foreign influence from the Middle East

Al-Qaida emerged in opposition to Soviet occupation of Afghanistan

First Islamic Revolution occurred in non-Arab Iran

2 | Al-Qaida and the Globalisation of Terror

In 1996 Bin Laden returned to Afghanistan where he was sheltered by the **Taliban** movement. He used his wealth to revive al-Qaida and build 'a *jihad* camp for the world'. He was joined in Afghanistan by Ayman al-Zawahari, often described (since then) as 'number two' to Bin Laden. Al-Zawahari was an Egyptian, trained as a doctor, with many years of experience in the struggle of Islamic radicals against the Egyptian government. He brought with him networks of Egyptian activists, hardened by years of struggle in Egypt, into the new organisation now called al-Qaida.

In the mid-1990s, the failure of the so-called 'peace process' between Israel and the Palestinians gave a further spur to the development of radical Islam, especially as there was no progress in gaining Jerusalem for the Palestinians or any recognition of

Key question
How and why did al-Qaida gain support in the 1990s?

Taliban
An Islamic movement, whose leaders were drawn from the former *mujahideen*, which took control of the Afghan government in 1996.

Key term

Key term

'Right to return'
The right of Palestinian refugees and their descendants to return to their pre-1948 homes in Israel and the occupied territories.

the **'right to return'** to their homeland for millions of Palestinian living in refugee camps. Worst of all, for the Palestinians, the Israelis continued to build Jewish settlements on Arab land on the West Bank (see page 100). In 1998, Bin Laden and al-Zawahari called on Muslims 'to fulfil their duty to kill Americans and their allies in order to liberate the al-Aqsa mosque in Jerusalem and the Holy Mosque [in Mecca] from their grip'. They listed three reasons for their jihad:

- the presence of US military bases in the Arabian peninsular
- the 'destruction' of Iraq by the USA (through the continuing use of sanctions)
- US backing for 'the petty state of the Jews' (i.e. Israel).

The Americans countered by saying that their military presence in Saudi Arabia and the Gulf states was to protect those states from threats posed by Iran and Iraq. However, film footage, on

Osama Bin Laden. He was widely respected in the Arab world for having given up a life of wealth and comfort for one of hardship and danger. He was (and still is) seen by many as a Middle Eastern Robin Hood, defending the poor and vulnerable against a distant tyrant.

television and the Internet, from Israel/Palestine and Iraq, convinced many Muslims that the USA was an enemy, not an ally. The continuing crisis in Israel/Palestine and the crippling effect of sanctions on Iraq (see page 133) ensured a steady stream of recruits to al-Qaida.

Al-Qaida targets the USA

The leaders of al-Qaida did not set out to build a mass protest movement or to fight elections. Instead, they relied on a small number of activists, loosely connected to each other, who often had little contact with the organisation's leaders so that it was difficult for the security services to penetrate them. As the twentieth century drew to a close, al-Qaida leaders had in their sights the one country that dominated the Middle East. Even 10 years after the end of the Gulf War to liberate Kuwait, the USA still had 25,000 troops in the region, 10,000 of them in Saudi Arabia and Kuwait. The Americans had two aircraft carriers in the Gulf, together with 15 warships and 350 fighter jets. They had yet more troops and planes on a huge military base in Turkey and they supplied billions of dollars' worth of military aid and weapons to Israel, Egypt, Turkey, Saudi Arabia and the smaller Gulf states. In the eyes of many living in the Middle East, it seemed like a deliberate design to dominate the Arab and Muslim world.

In the late 1990s, members of al-Qaida embarked on a number of spectacular attacks on US targets:

- In 1996, a truck bomb targeted a US military barracks in Saudi Arabia, killing or injuring nearly 400 Americans.
- In 1998, 19 suicide 'martyrs' bombed the US embassies in Kenya and Tanzania, killing 12 American diplomats and 200 Africans.
- In 2000, a boat packed with explosives rammed the side of the USS *Cole*, a destroyer, off the coast of Yemen, killing 17 American sailors.

'9/11': The attack on the World Trade Center in New York 2001

On 11 September 2001, 19 men hijacked four US passenger planes and flew two of them into the twin towers of the World Trade Center in New York and one into the Pentagon, the US defence centre, in Washington DC. A fourth plane crashed in Pennsylvania. Over 3000 people were killed. The majority of Muslims were appalled. The Koran teaches that the only just war is a war of self-defence. But Osama Bin Laden and his followers claimed (and still do) that Muslims *were* under attack – in Arabia, in Iraq, in Palestine – and that the US supported corrupt and oppressive governments such as that of Saudi Arabia, from where most of the '9/11' bombers originated. Nevertheless, although millions of Arabs felt angry and bitter after years of humiliation by the West, the methods of '9/11' caused revulsion. Even the Iranian President, who was no friend of the USA, condemned what he saw as the bombers' un-Islamic methods.

Key question
What targets did al-Qaida select for bombing?

Key question
What was the impact of '9/11'?

Key date
'9/11' attacks on New York and Washington: September 2001

Key dates

US attack on Afghanistan: October 2001

US invasion of Iraq: 2003

The US government took stock before launching its 'war on terror'. President Bush was quick to proclaim that Islam was a great and peaceful religion and he visited American mosques to show his support for American Muslims. Then, in October, US forces attacked Afghanistan and overthrew the Taliban government that had provided a safe haven for al-Qaida. They did not catch Bin Laden who was quick to taunt Bush for failing to destroy him: he did this in a video message broadcast on the Arabic satellite television channel, al-Jazeera. Al-Qaida later took responsibility for the bombing of Madrid railway station, which killed 191 people in 2004, and for the London bombings in 2005, which killed 52. (While al-Qaida might have inspired the London bombings it is not thought that al-Qaida operatives organised them.)

When US forces drove Iraqi forces out of Kuwait in 1991, they had much support in the Arab world. But when the USA invaded Iraq in 2003, their 'war on terror' was seen by many in the Middle East as a war on Islam, especially when Bush declared that 'you're either with us or against us'. Meanwhile, Israeli tanks moved into the West Bank (see page 103) to crush the Palestinian *Intifada*. The subsequent mass protests that took place in many parts of the Arab world shook the Arab governments that were linked to the USA. Today, the 'Palestinian problem', what Muslims see as the injustice suffered by the Palestinians, remains at the heart of the conflict in the Middle East (see page 108).

For most people in the West, the world changed on 11 September 2001. Westerners could no longer assume that events in the Middle East did not concern them. What happens in Gaza or on the West Bank, in Iraq or in Afghanistan today is likely to affect people in the West tomorrow. What many Muslims see as the West's occupation of Muslim lands has given rise to terrorism both within the Middle East and in the wider world.

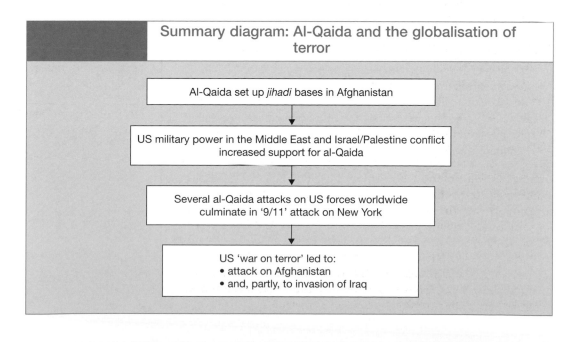

Summary diagram: Al-Qaida and the globalisation of terror

Al-Qaida set up *jihadi* bases in Afghanistan

↓

US military power in the Middle East and Israel/Palestine conflict increased support for al-Qaida

↓

Several al-Qaida attacks on US forces worldwide culminate in '9/11' attack on New York

↓

US 'war on terror' led to:
- attack on Afghanistan
- and, partly, to invasion of Iraq

Study Guide

In the style of Edexcel

To what extent does the Iranian Revolution of 1979 account for the growth of political Islam in the Middle East?

Exam tips

The cross-references are intended to take you straight to the material that will help you to answer the question.

Start by re-reading pages 118–20 of Chapter 7 and all of Chapter 9.

For this essay you need to assess the impact of the Islamic Revolution in Iran, and then the impact of *other* factors, on the growth of political Islam. Then, finally, make a judgement of how important the Iranian Revolution was in comparison to the other factors.

First, briefly explain what the Iranian Revolution achieved (i.e. the establishment of an Islamic state) and what this meant (pages 118–20). Then assess its impact on the wider Middle East, including the taking of US hostages. You will need to identify the limits of its impact as well, explaining the suspicions of the largely Sunni, Arab states and peoples. The revolutionary government in Iran was keen to spread its revolution: did the Iran–Iraq War inspire the growth of political Islam beyond Iran? If not, why not (pages 120–3)?

Other factors considered could include:

- The decline of Arab nationalism and its perceived failure in defending the Arab, Muslim world against the impact of the West and of Israel in particular (page 142).
- The appeal of political Islam as the best way to renew the Muslim world and expel foreign domination.
- The impact of defeat against Israel in 1967 and Egypt's peace with Israel in 1979.
- Most important of all, the emergence of al-Qaida in Afghanistan and then its later impact in Arab states like Egypt and Saudi Arabia (pages 144–6).
- The effects of the continuing Israeli–Palestinian conflict and of the US military presence in the Gulf in fuelling support for Islamic fundamentalism.
- The development of the al-Qaida network and its international bombing campaign. You might also refer to the growth of Islamic groups like Hamas and Hizbollah, the latter certainly supported by Iran (page 107).

In conclusion, you need to weigh up the importance of the Iranian revolution in relation to these other factors (and there may be some overlap, as in the case of Hizbollah's growth).

The very best answers will have weighed one factor against another as the essay developed. All the way through, therefore, there will have been mini-conclusions, so the conclusion at the very end will not be the only point at which the relative evaluation took place. Rather, it will complete the argument that ran through the whole essay.

Glossary

Al-Qaida From the Arabic word meaning a base (e.g. for training recruits in Afghanistan), it came to refer to an organisation, or a network, of Islamists of whom Osama Bin Laden was the leader. Responsible for the attacks on New York and Washington in 2001.

Anti-Semitism Feelings or actions showing prejudice or hatred towards the Jews.

Appease To make concessions in order to avoid conflict.

Arab Higher Committee A committee of Palestinian Arab leaders.

Arab League A body established in 1945 to represent the Arab states.

Arab Legion The army of Transjordan.

Arab nationalism A movement striving for Arab political unity.

Armistice An agreement to stop fighting.

Ayatollah Among Shia Muslims, the Ayatollahs are the most senior scholars, experts in interpreting the Koran.

Baath Means 'Renaissance' or rebirth of Arab power. The Baath Party had originally been established in Syria in the 1950s but its influence extended to several Arab countries.

Baghdad Pact An alliance formed by Britain, Turkey, Iran and, later, Pakistan and Iraq. Its headquarters were in the Iraqi capital of Baghdad.

Black September A Palestinian group which killed 11 Israeli athletes at the 1972 Olympics.

Blockade The blocking of a place or region by troops or ships to prevent goods or people reaching it.

Brinkmanship Pursuing a dangerous policy to the limits of safety.

Camp David The US President's mountain retreat.

Charisma The capacity to inspire devotion in others, as if endowed with superhuman or, at least, exceptional powers.

CIA The US Central Intelligence Agency, responsible for gathering information about foreign governments for the US government.

Coalition A union of two or more groups for a specific purpose.

Coalition Provisional Authority An organisation set up by the USA and its coalition allies to govern Iraq.

Cold War A state of tension, but not actual war, that existed between the USA and the Soviet Union between the late 1940s and late 1980s.

Coup Sudden or violent change of government.

'Crimes against humanity' Widespread or systematic attack against a civilian population.

Curfew A time or signal after which it was compulsory for people to remain indoors.

Diaspora The dispersal of Jews in many different parts of the world.

Eretz Israel The Land of Israel, as in the Bible. In effect, this meant the whole of

Palestine, not just the area allocated to the Jewish state by the UN.

Fatah   A Palestinian guerrilla group founded by Yasser Arafat. Its general strategy was to drag the Arab states into war with Israel so that a Palestinian state might be established.

Fedayeen   Men trained to carry out raids (literally, 'those who sacrifice themselves').

'Green line'   The border between Israel and the West Bank before the 1967 Six-Day War.

Guerrillas   Soldiers who avoid fighting in open battle when possible; they prefer to use tactics like ambushes and hit-and-run raids.

Haganah   The Jewish Defence Force, which was set up in the 1920s and was later to form the basis of the Israeli army.

Hamas   Founded in Gaza in 1988 by Sheikh Ahmed Yassin, a religious teacher. The movement opposed the Oslo Accords and refused to recognise the state of Israel.

High Commissioner   The most senior diplomat, like an ambassador, representing the British government.

Hizbollah   A radical Islamic group based in southern Lebanon.

Imperialism   Rule by one nation or people over another.

Insurgency   An uprising to try and overthrow a government.

'International communism'   A term used by the US government to describe the threat posed by the communist Soviet Union and its allies during the Cold War.

Intifada   The Palestinian uprising that erupted in Gaza and the West Bank in 1987.

Irgun   A small secret Zionist organisation which fought for a Jewish state in all of Palestine.

Islamic fundamentalism   The belief that the state should be based wholly on Islamic law, as in Muhammad's day.

Islamists   Those who believe in political Islam.

Israeli Defence Force (IDF)   The Israeli armed forces, most of whose members had been in the Haganah.

Israelites   The name by which Jews were known in ancient times, hence the 'Land of Israel' was their Promised Land.

Jewish Agency   The governing body of the Zionist movement in Palestine during the British mandate.

Jihad   An Arabic word meaning 'struggle', both internal and personal (against sin) and external (against threats to Muslim lands).

Kibbutzim   Settlements in Israel where people live and work together.

Koran   The holy book of the Muslims which, they believe, contains the word of God as conveyed to the Prophet Muhammad in the seventh century AD.

Kurds   The Kurds are Muslims but not Arab. They form about 20 per cent of the Iraqi population and are concentrated in the north of the country.

Lobbied   To lobby is to win the support of members of a law-making body (e.g. the US Congress) so as to shape its policy.

Mandate   An order or a command, in this case from the League of Nations, giving Britain and France control of Arab lands previously ruled by Turkey. Britain and France were to prepare the Arab lands for eventual self-government.

Martial law   Military government, with ordinary law suspended.

Martyr   Someone who dies or suffers greatly for a cause, especially for religious beliefs. There is a particularly strong tradition of martyrdom among Shiites.

Militant   A person who supports the use of force.

Muhammad   Born in the Arabian city of Mecca in AD 572. For Muslims, he is the messenger and prophet of God.

Mujahideen   An Arabic word meaning 'those who struggle', for example in a *jihad*, or holy war.

Mullah   The title given to some Muslim clergy.

Nakbah   An Arabic word for 'catastrophe' or 'disaster', used to refer to the 1948–9 war and the creation of the Palestinian refugee problem.

Nationalise   To transfer from private to government ownership.

'No-fly zones'   These were areas in the Kurdish north and, later, the Shiite south where Iraqi planes were forbidden to fly. They were designed to protect these areas from attack by Saddam's army. The zones were policed by US and British planes which flew from bases in Turkey or from aircraft carriers in the Gulf.

Non-aligned   The non-aligned nations were those that did not wish to step into line with either the West (the USA and its allies) or with the Soviet Union and its allies.

Occupied territories   Lands controlled by the troops of a foreign power (in this case, the West Bank, Gaza, Sinai and Golan Heights, all occupied by Israeli troops).

Oslo Accord   The name given to the agreement resulting from peace negotiations held in Oslo.

Ottoman   The name of the Turkish dynasty, named after its founder, Osman. In the sixteenth century, the Turkish empire conquered much of south-east Europe and the Middle East.

Palestine Liberation Organisation (PLO)   As well as leading the armed struggle to regain Palestine, the PLO provided many health and welfare services in the Palestinian refugee camps. The Red Crescent society, which set up and ran hospitals, was headed by Yasser Arafat's brother.

Palestinian Authority   A Palestinian 'government', with limited authority, in the West Bank and Gaza.

Palestinian Front for the Liberation of Palestine (PFLP)   An organisation set up by George Habash, a Palestinian Christian. It carried out many terrorist acts.

Partition   Division into two or more parts.

Persecution   Punishment or cruel treatment, often because of ethnicity or religion.

Political Islam   A political movement which asserts that Islam is the solution to the problems of the modern world. Its followers advocate Islamic states where the Koran is the basis of government and society.

'Promised Land'   The land of Palestine (which Jews believed God had promised to them).

'Regime change'   Change in the system of government (in this case, Saddam's dictatorship).

Reparations   Damages or compensation which Germany paid to Israel for the persecution of the Jews during the Second World War.

Repatriate   To send people back to their own country.

Reprisal   An act of retaliation against an enemy to stop them from doing something again.

Republic   A country whose head of state is not a monarch.

Revisionist   A 'revised' interpretation based on a critical re-examination of historical facts.

'Right to return'   The right of Palestinian refugees and their descendants to return to their pre-1948 homes in Israel and the occupied territories.

Secular   Not religious or spiritual: a secular state is one not based on religion.

Settlement   A group of houses, as built by the Israelis on the West Bank and in Gaza.

Shah   The title of the King or Emperor of Iran. It is similar to Tsar, the name of the Russian monarch, or Kaiser, the German emperor.

Soviet Union   The name by which communist Russia was known from 1917 to 1991. Its official name was the Union of Soviet Socialist Republics (USSR).

Stern gang   A Zionist terrorist group founded in 1939.

Synagogue   A building where Jews worship.

Taliban   An Islamic movement, whose leaders were drawn from the former *mujahideen*, which took control of the Afghan government in 1996.

'The axis of evil'   A phrase used by US President Bush to describe the link he saw between the states that he regarded as enemies.

Trade sanctions   A form of punishment where the UN bans a country from trading with other countries in order to force it to obey a UN resolution.

UN General Assembly   The main body of the UN in which every state is represented.

United Arab Republic   The union of Egypt and Syria formed in 1958.

United Nations Security Council   The most important body in the UN, it can take action against a country either by imposing sanctions or by using UN troops.

UNSCOM   UN special committee set up to search for and destroy Iraq's WMD.

Vietnam   The USA had a large military force fighting against communist North Vietnam and its communist allies in South Vietnam.

War of attrition   A war in which each side tries to wear the other out.

Weapons of mass destruction (WMD)   Biological, chemical or nuclear weapons, used to kill as many people as possible.

White Paper   A government document making recommendations for discussion.

Yom Kippur   Day of Atonement, an important Jewish religious day of fasting and an annual Jewish holiday.

Zionists   Those who advocated the creation of a Jewish homeland and, later, an independent state, in Palestine.

Index